CW00556635

The History of
Johnson & Sons Ltd
of Great Yarmouth

For Jamie

The History of
Johnson & Sons Ltd
of Great Yarmouth

Ann Green

First published May 2013 by

Holm Oak Publishing,

24 Church View, Holton, Halesworth, Suffolk IP19 8PB

British Library Cataloguing in Publication Data.

A catalogue record for this book is available from the British Library.

ISBN 9780953340668

Printed by Barnwell Print Ltd

Aylsham, Norfolk NR11 6SU

Also by Ann Green (as Ann Gander) :

Top Hats & Servants' Tales: A Century of Life

on Somerleyton Estate

Adrian Bell: Voice of the Countryside

The Story of the Southwold-Walberswick Ferry

(with Dani Church)

Contents

Acknowledgements

My sincere thanks to David Johnson, the last surviving member of the family who worked at Johnson & Sons Ltd, and who kindly shared his memories and collection of historical documents and catalogues. Also thanks to the Reverend Dr Malcolm Johnson for invaluable family history research, photos, information and advice, and to Ann Bond for details about her father Gordon.

I am grateful to Paul Johnson and Susan Herbert for the delightful photos and tales of their father Noel, and to all members of the extended Johnson family who gave help, support and interest in the project.

To all the former members of staff and their families who contributed photos and precious memories – I am much in their debt and I hope that I have done justice to their stories in the limited space available. I apologise if I have unintentionally missed out anyone or anything or have omitted a credit where due – in a few cases a photographer or original source could not be traced.

Special thanks to Joy Hawkins who had rescued a number of documents and artefacts from destruction, and who shared her wonderful collection of photos. Also to Pauline Edwards for sharing her own memoirs, to June Willison, Ronnie Webb, Frank and Pam Greenwood, and Doris Porter, and to Ann Johnson and Margaret Jay, relations of the Gooda family who supplied superb background information and photos; to Ken Houghton and many others for pictures of the factories and John Winterburn for background about the hosiery factory.

A huge 'thank you' to everyone who made contact and to those who agreed to be interviewed, and whose stories brought the book to life.

My thanks to Christopher Knights, Chairman and Managing Director of Yarmouth Stores Ltd – the history of his own family firm was entwined with that of Johnson & Sons Ltd for a time, and I am grateful for having been allowed access to their impressive archives.

My gratitude also to Archant Newspapers and in particular Anne Edwards, Editor of the Great Yarmouth Mercury, for permission to reproduce quotations and photos from that excellent local newspaper which has recorded the milestones of the Johnson & Sons story. Their coverage of my appeal for former Johnson's employees to make contact brought forward a host of new memories and material.

Finally my appreciation to my partner John and my sons Matthew and Jamie for support, encouragement, dinners and dog-walking.

EXTRACT OF JOHNSON FAMILY TREE

Showing key members associated with the firm

Robert Johnson m Sarah Knowles
(1770 - 1855)

John Johnson   m   Elizabeth Smith
(1795 – 1878)

John William Johnson   m Caroline Thomasine Budds
(1823 – 1902)

Frederick J. B. Johnson
(1847 – 1891)

Arthur Herbert Johnson
(1849 – 1917)
m Charlotte Muffett

Charles W. Johnson
(1859 - ?)

John William Budds Johnson
(1845 – 1908)
m Elizabeth Leggett

Edwin Horace
(1881 - 1953)
m Gertrude Beeching

Oswald Charles
(1882 – 1944)
m2 Marj Cranswick

William James
(1873 - 1934)

John 'Jack' Arthur
(1884 – 1944)

Frank Arthur
(1875 – 1946)
m1 Annie Maud Wright

Michael
(1917 – 1961)

John Noel
(1923 - 2005)

Davic
(1926 -)

Russell Frank A.
(1909 – 1978)

Gordon Herbert
(1912 – 1978)

Chapter One

Who started it?

For about a hundred years, the clothing firm Johnson & Sons was a household name in Great Yarmouth, and it was a well-known brand much further afield - even worldwide. A set of Johnson's oilskins could be found hanging on a peg in countless fishermen's homes, in the rooms of Scottish herring girls, on board merchant vessels and British warships.

In a town like Yarmouth which depended heavily on the sea for employment, almost everyone probably knew somebody who owned at least one garment made by Johnson & Sons or was working in a factory that made them. Whole families found jobs at Johnson's. Such was the influence of this family firm in the mid 19th to 20th centuries: they were one of the largest employers in the area, and their part in the social history of the town was significant.

Illustration from 1913 Johnson & Sons catalogue

A number of articles have been written about the firm and its history, and various different members of the family have been credited with having founded the business. No doubt it grew, as so many successful businesses have, from small beginnings. However there is some doubt about exactly when it came into being; the claim that it started as far back as 1801 may have been a harmless marketing ploy, which stuck.

Below: Cover of 1905 catalogue and price list stating that the firm was established in 1801

In the early 19th century Great Yarmouth was poised to become a popular seaside resort but for now its fortunes still rested largely on its significance as a port. Not only was there a thriving fishing industry but merchant ships and sometimes military ships brought sailors onto the land and into the crowded, narrow streets and alleyways, or rows, swelling the population, which in 1801 was counted as being just under 15,000. Shops, public houses and small industries of all kinds burgeoned as local entrepreneurs took advantage of the demand for goods and services, and catered for them.

Family tradition has it that a Johnson ancestor first took over a small premises by the fish docks and sold chandlery, only later turning to manufacturing clothing. However written sources have tended to suggest that the earlier Johnson – there is disagreement over which one – began trading in garments from the start.

According to one magazine article[1] it would have been John Johnson senior who first started the business of producing weather-resistant clothing for seamen, and it says 'from the beginning the firm catered exclusively for the wants of those who go down to the sea in ships, making specialities of oilskin clothing, and afterwards of hand knit guernseys, and so gradually increasing the scope and number of their departments as one success led to another.'

However, another newspaper cutting from about 1950 gives the precise year of foundation as 1801, and this definite date was carried forward until it became a staple claim on the company's literature. In 1801 John Johnson was just six years old; so if the date is genuine it must have been his father who first had the idea.

John Johnson was born to Robert and Sarah Johnson on 7th April 1795 and he was baptised in the St Nicholas parish of Great Yarmouth. His parents lived in the claustrophobic environment of the Rows – first in 81 and later in Row 21. His father Robert was a shoemaker, who was then aged 24 and Sarah was five years older. She had signed her name

---

[1] *The Textile Trade Review* Dec 1894 p8 stated the founder was the grandfather of the then directors

with a cross on the marriage register six months earlier on 6th October 1794.

With insufficient records of the countless tradesmen in the town at that time, we cannot know for sure who it was that first started to offer protective clothing for the fishermen and merchant seamen who frequented Yarmouth harbour. However there were producers of oilskin in the town and as a shoemaker Robert would have had the skills to cut and stitch the thick greasy fabric; it is possible that he started to do so as a sideline to his main profession. His son John followed the same trade.

In 1811 soon after John's 16th birthday he enlisted in the Army, in the 28th Foot Regiment – later the Gloucester Regiment - 'for life.' His service record[2] describes him as '5ft 2ins, fair complexion, grey eyes and dark brown hair.' His profession was given as cordwainer – or shoemaker. He served at barracks in Devon and in Cork and in 1814 he is recorded as spending the Autumn guarding French and American prisoners of war at Dartmoor. In the following year his regiment travelled to Ostend, armed with muskets and rifles in preparation for war against Napoleon. He saw action with the Duke of Wellington's forces in June that year, and although initially outnumbered the allied troops won what would become known as The Battle of Waterloo, with heavy losses on both sides.

Somehow Private John Johnson came through it all; he is listed as taking part in the July victory parade, marching down the Champs Elysees. He received his Waterloo medal in 1816 but then suffered several bouts of ill health and was discharged on medical grounds in 1821.

Records show that in April 1822 John Johnson married Elizabeth Smith, a tailoress. At the time of the 1841 census they were living in Row 36 with their seven children and John Johnson still declared that he was a shoemaker by trade. At this point there had been no mention of either John or his father Robert creating or selling items of clothing, and

---

[2] National Archives ref WO97/472/140

no reference to working with oilskins. Possibly they may have done so on a small scale, but it appears that John was in no position to be embarking on new business ventures.

In 1851, still living at the same address in the Rows, John was recorded as being a Chelsea Pensioner. The rate he received in 1859 was 6d a day. Later that year he appears to have moved to the Chelsea Barracks; however his wife Elizabeth was unable to join him and she stayed behind at their home which was now in Jury Street, Great Yarmouth. She is recorded there in 1861, incorrectly as a widow, living with her daughter Elvina who was also a dressmaker. In the 1871 census John was still an inmate at the Chelsea Barracks and Elizabeth was living in Hackney with her daughter and a granddaughter, however the family moved back to Norfolk soon afterwards. John died in Great Yarmouth in 1878 and Elizabeth passed away the following year. They are buried together at the Kitchener Road Cemetery in their home town.

John and Elizabeth Johnson had raised seven children, the eldest being John William Johnson, born in January 1823. He is the one most often cited as having started the family business and it does seem to have risen to prominence during his lifetime. According to the second newspaper article, 'By 1850 it occupied various small buildings in the Middlegate area but even then fewer than 50 people were employed.'

It is thought that as well as making protective clothing from oilskin material, Johnson's bought knitted sweaters made by the Scottish women who came every year to process fish in the herring season.

John junior had lived with his parents in Row 36 until July 1844 when he made a valuable and lasting match with Caroline Thomasine Budds who had also been born in Great Yarmouth; her family were sail makers and it is said that they had connections in Whitechapel, dealing in oils and tallow. Not only did Caroline give birth to fourteen children – sadly a number of them died in infancy - but it is likely that her husband and her father discussed their businesses and John saw opportunities to branch out from his humble beginnings as a shoemaker's son.

Ship building was big business in the town and at this time there were about 550 vessels registered at the port, excluding fishing smacks and small craft. During the Autumn an estimated 1,600 men were engaged in the herring fishing, with six to seven hundred men and women employed in the curing houses, and many more in ancillary work.[3] There were literally thousands of people in need of clothing that could help keep out the worst of the weather.

Those who worked alongside the fishermen included the Scottish girls who came to gut and pack the herring – they too needed protective clothing for this filthy work.

---

[3] Pigot's Directory of Norfolk 1839 p517

In the 1851 census John William Johnson, his wife and three small children were living at 56 Belgrave Place. John was recorded as being a draper by profession. From now on the Johnsons would be going up in the world and they appear to have moved house every few years. In 1861 they were at 100 King Street with their growing family and, significantly, they were now able to employ a house servant and a nurse.

John first appears in the local *Post Office Directory* in 1865 as a linen draper; three years later he is listed in the *Harrods Postal and Commercial Directory* of Norfolk and Norwich thus: 'Johnson – John Wm wholesale south-wester & oil cloth manufacturer and retail general outfitter, 26 Gaol Street.' Finally it is confirmed that a Johnson was trading in oilskin clothing.

John William and Caroline Johnson

John William Johnson was the first real entrepreneur of the family and so perhaps it does seem in retrospect that those other accounts of the Johnson firm having started in 1801 were a little exaggerated. It is he who can be traced as operating a proper business from the 1860s onwards, and it was he who expanded the range of goods sold. In the 1871 census John reported his profession as Manufacturing Outfitter. Naturally, he hoped his sons would follow him.

The couple's first son, John William Budds Johnson (1845-1908) appears to have been schooled and then sent away by the age of 15 to work as a clerk in a London warehouse, possibly associated with the Johnsons' firm.[4] He returned, married and joined the business. Two of his own sons would later join too.

Frederick James Budds Johnson (1847-1891) also went into the business: in the 1881 census he was living with his wife and children in Yarmouth and declared his profession to be 'Oil clothing manufacturer employing 21 men, 5 boys and 24 girls'. This accords with the article which suggested the company was employing up to 50 people, although at an earlier stage.

Arthur Herbert Johnson (1849-1917) would be instrumental in taking the company from strength to strength during his time there, with his own sons and grandsons following in his footsteps.

The two youngest boys did not take such an active part in running the family business: Charles Walter (1859-?) went away to London to learn the art of auctioneering and returned to Norfolk where he married and worked as an auctioneer throughout his career, although he did become a shareholder of Johnson's. Tragically, his only son Russell was killed at Gallipoli in the First World War.

Henry Alfred (1866-1918), known as Harry, became a butcher by trade; he married and raised a family, moving away to Cambridgeshire.

---

[4] 1861 census shows JWB Johnson lodging in Bread Street, London

White's Directory of 1883 has the following entry: 'Johnson J. W. & Sons Sou'wester & oil clothing manufacturer & fishermen's outfitters 26 Middlegate Street & 70 South Quay.' This speaks volumes – John William Johnson had formally taken his sons into the business, and they were expanding fast, with more than one factory site. They were about to enter a period of further development and prosperity that John's father and grandfather, brought up in the cramped, slum-like conditions of the Rows, surely could not have dreamed about.

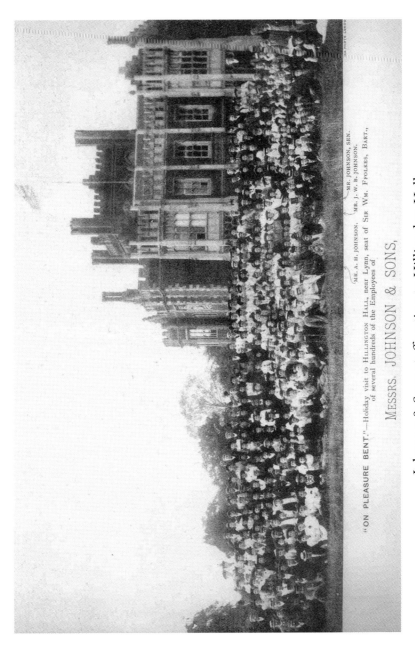

Johnson & Sons staff outing to Hillingdon Hall
Photograph fromTextile Trade Review December 1894

Chapter Two

From strength to strength

In March 1885 the *London Gazette* published the announcement that John William Johnson had retired from the partnership of J.W. Johnson & Sons, and from then on the business would be run by John William Budds Johnson, Frederick James Budds Johnson and Arthur Herbert Johnson. The firm was described as being 'Clothiers, Drapers and Manufacturers of Waterproof Clothing.'

The father and sons team had taken the leap from attracting custom purely from sea-going types to land-based workers in need of tough, durable outfits. They were supplying outfits to bargemen who plied the inland waterways, and to engineers and firemen, among many others. Since the coming of the railway in 1844, new opportunities had arisen to send orders to retailers, and many more people were being brought in to visit Great Yarmouth. With leisure and tourism growing in the town, Johnson's was also tapping in to the market for weatherproof clothing for the yachting community.

Now the younger generation of Johnsons could develop ambitious new outlets, including selling their products abroad. The article in the *Textile Trade Review* of December 1894 starts under the heading 'Eminent Manufacturing Firms – an unique speciality house' and continues 'Messrs Johnson & Sons, manufacturers and shippers of oil clothing, hosiery, seamen's clothing etc. Factories: Great Yarmouth. London Warehouse: 10 Gutter Lane, E.C.'

It said that the company had evolved, improving their goods year after year and adding new departments; 'In this process of evolution the one generation took up the final achievements of the last as vantage ground for continued and accelerated progress, until today the firm, possessing as it does all the experience and improvements of nearly 100 years, is probably the largest and best of the kind in the world.'

There is a list of the garments that were now being manufactured by Johnson & Sons: '...every conceivable kind of Oilskin Clothing for Seamen and Fishermen in Sou'westers, Coats, Trousers, Leggings, Jackets, Sleeves, Shirts, Aprons etc... The Hosiery Department is also one of the most important – their Hand-knit Guernseys and Mittens and their Boot, Alloa, and Black Worsted Knicker Hose and Ribs having attained an unique celebrity. Their Cardigan Jackets, Jerseys, Franklins and Guernseys are well known makes all over the world. Yachting Caps, Trousers, and Jumpers, Navy Dungaree and Bluette Jackets and Trousers, Cotton Jackets, all kinds of Serge Jackets, Trousers and Suits, Fearnought and Duffell Trousers and Doppers; Kersey Drawers, Singlets, Serge Suits, Boys', Youths' and Men's Ready-mades in Pilots, Beavers and Diagonals; Fancy Printed Moles, Quilts etc...'

These quaintly named items, most of which are now the forgotten garments of an adventurous, industrious and practical age, were just a fraction of the range of clothing that Johnson's now had to offer.

The article states that the factories of the firm 'are fitted with all the latest improvements suggested by modern invention,' including steam-driven machinery. The manufacturing plant had recently been expanded, it said, and the London warehouse had been taken on to store large quantities of stock. The Yarmouth addresses given in *Kelly's Directory* of 1883 were 26 Middlegate Street and 70 South Quay. Less than ten years later the directory showed them at Middlegate Street, at 70, 71 and 72 South Quay and at 8 South Gates Road. By 1912 they had taken over 69 South Quay as well, and occupied 26, 33, 34, 35, 36 and 37 South Gates Road as well as the premises in Middlegate Street.

With hundreds of women being employed in hand knitting as well as all those operating the sewing machines, and counting the men who used the lethal cutting machines and serviced the boilers, engines and mechanical equipment plus those packing and despatching, it was estimated that 2000 workers were now being employed. The Johnsons appreciated the value of their staff and arranged entertainments and outings for them, like the one shown in the photograph that accompanied the *Textile Trade Review* article. It said they also took 'a deep personal interest in the moral, social, and material welfare of their employees, each of whom is individually known to them.' The latter may, again, have been a slight exaggeration.

By the closing years of the 19th century Johnson & Sons had excelled in the production of high quality protective clothing, and their efforts had been recognised all over the world. They were able to boast 'Eight Prize Medals Awarded,' and their letter heading was adorned with the proof of their haul: one from the Maritime and Piscatorial Exhibition at the London Royal Aquarium in 1877; two from the National Fisheries Exhibition in Norwich, 1881; two from the exhibition in London, 1883, and from the Great International Fisheries Exhibition in Sweden in the same year; two from the International Fisheries Exhibition at Edinburgh, 1882; a silver medal in Sydney and a Highest Award from Melbourne in 1888.

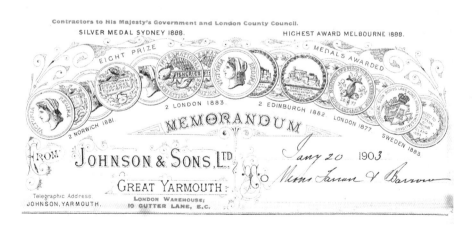

Letter heading with images of the awards

Johnson's stand at a trade exhibition, possibly London 1883

The catalogue entry for the London Exhibition of 1883 reveals that Johnson & Sons were offering:

i.   Life saving apparel
ii. Every description of Waterproof oil clothing, as worn by Fishermen of the British Isles and other parts of the world
iii. Waterproof Oil Clothing for Captains, Sailors, and Pilots.
iv. Sou'Westers for all parts of the world
v.   Every description of Fishermen's Clothing, other than Waterproof, for sea and shore service
vi. Water Boots of all lengths
vii. Life-saving Garments, as worn by Life-boat Crews and Fishermen engaged in ferrying Fish from smack to carrier

viii. Waterproof Oil Clothing in all Garments for ladies and gentlemen Yachting and Fishing

ix. Ladies' Waterproof Oil Cloak fitted with Life-Saving Apparatus.[5]

There was plenty of scope for new members of the Johnson family to take their place in the firm and William James, son of John William Budds Johnson, became a partner in March 1895, at the age of 22. To celebrate, a dinner was held for staff at the Brunswick Hotel, with roast meats, puddings and pastries followed by numerous toasts: to the Queen, to the three partners John, Arthur and William Johnson, to the firm and to the staff. Finally there was a toast to 'the visitors' who were Messrs G.W. Chadd and S. Julier.

No doubt there were similar festivities when Arthur's son Frank entered the firm, in about 1896. He was followed later by his brothers Edwin and Oswald. Tragically, John's second son George would not follow – he contracted consumption in his youth and was sent to South Africa in the hope that his health would improve, but he died there in about 1897, aged 20. A third son, John 'Jack' Arthur did enter the firm later but the fourth, Edward, was unwell for some years and was nursed at home before dying at the age of 23.

It became clear that the next logical step in developing the business was to turn it into a Limited Company, enabling the directors to attract investment and share the increasing profits. The Memorandum and Articles of Association for Johnson & Sons Ltd were drawn up by Yarmouth solicitors Wiltshire & Son, and dated 1st February 1898. The capital was set at £75,000 in £1 shares and the first subscribers were John William Budds Johnson, his wife Eliza and son William; Arthur Herbert, his wife Charlotte and son Frank, and Charles Walter Johnson, the auctioneer. Their brother Frederick had died at the early age of 44.

---

[5] The Fisheries Exhibition Literature Vol 1 London, W Clowes 1883

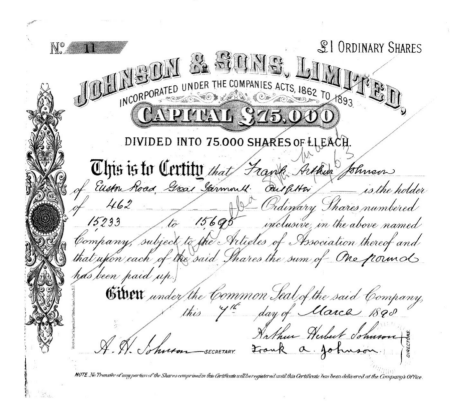

Certificate of shares held by Frank Johnson

Only John and Arthur, and their sons William and Frank were to be the directors; John was the first chairman and Arthur took the role of managing director, requiring him to hold at least £5,000 of the share capital in the company. In return he was to receive a salary of £800 a year, equivalent to almost £60,000 today, as well as the dividends on his shares.

The addresses now occupied by the firm were in Middlegate Street, in Rows 104, 108 and 110, in Admiralty Road, and they still had the London warehouse in Gutter Lane, along with premises in Liskeard,

Cornwall. The objects of the company were to carry on business as manufacturers of oilskin, rubber and waterproof clothing, hosiery and goods of all kinds; also to carry on business as general outfitters, clothiers and drapers, warehousemen, ship chandlers and, rather oddly, as fruit and potato merchants.

Now on a very sound footing with regard to finance and their personal liability, the directors were able to invest and expand their activities further still. As a side venture they joined with local business associates William George Knights and George Wesley Chadd to form The Yarmouth Stores, with retail outlets in Yarmouth, Gorleston and Lowestoft. Naturally the stores sold Johnson's waterproof clothing as well as chandlery, tobacco and, again somewhat incompatibly, groceries and vegetables. Presumably their aim was to be a 'one stop shop' for all that seagoing folk could need, apart from rum. A brief account of the Yarmouth Stores history is given in Appendix Three.

Johnson's shop transferred to Yarmouth Stores

Only two old accounts books from the period 1898 to 1910 still survive, and they offer an interesting glimpse of the breadth of the firm's dealings. It is no surprise that some of the major purchases were from the Singer Sewing Machine Company and in 1898 Johnson's were trading-in some of the old machines they had been using, valued at 10/- each, and having others repaired: in 1909, 14 new machines were purchased at just under £6 each, they were of the 31K industrial variety, capable of sewing leather. Twelve were allocated to 'Miss Thompson's Room' and one to 'Miss Watson's Room' with one kept as spare. Replacement belts were bought regularly.

A great deal of maintenance and modification work was carried out by Thomas Lepard's engineering company of Cobholm. Further mechanisation was undertaken in the factories, with purchases of eyelet hole machines, special machines for sewing shirt buttons, 'crescent' cloth cutting machines (expensive at £60 each), automatic knife sharpeners, a steam press, as well as rollers, pulleys, cylinders and dials. The era of hand-knitting had come to an end, with several purchases of machines from the Harrison Knitting Machine Company of Manchester.

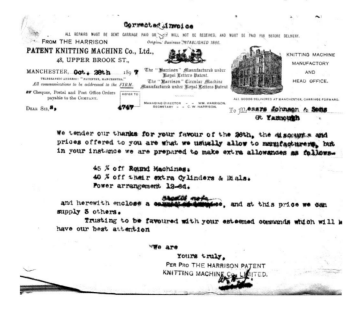

Agreements from September 1900 onwards show Johnson & Sons hiring machines from the International Button-Hole Sewing Machine Company, at a cost of £20 per annum. Large investments in new machinery and gas engines from Lepard of Cobholm were made in 1903, mainly for the factories at Middlegate Street and at Gorleston. Also in 1903 a coating machine was acquired to assist in applying dressing to the fabrics, although a great deal of the waterproofing process would continue to be carried out by hand for years to come.

Originally 'oilskin' had been produced by coating linen with linseed oil; it was sticky and heavy and over time the fabric tended to become stiff and yellow. John William Johnson had visited New Zealand where manufacturers were experimenting with new methods and by the late 1880s they had discovered that paraffin wax made a very good and much drier-feeling alternative. Johnson came back and created the 'NZ' line of waterproofs. Unfortunately he failed to patent the idea and John Barbour of South Shields discovered the same process. Barbour's wax jackets would become renowned worldwide.

Machinery used in the wax proofing process, Admiralty Road factory

In 1953 a journalist visited the oilskin works in Yarmouth and noted that the base fabric was grey calico, to which several applications of dressing were applied, with drying time allowed in between each layer. He wrote, 'Skilled workers apply a specially prepared oilskin dressing entirely by hand, many years of experience having proved that this is the only method of ensuring absolute waterproofedness. The garments are then treated with a mixture of shellac and ammonia on a hot polishing plate in order to remove "tackiness." This factory turns out an equivalent of 2,000 oilskin coats a week.'

The accounts show that in the early 1900s there were two main sewing rooms in the Yarmouth factory, presided over by Miss Thompson and Miss Watson. In Miss Thompson's room there were numerous Singer machines, also a quilting machine, while Miss Watson's room was described as the finishing room: there were Singer sewing machines, a zigzag machine and machines for creating flat felled seams of the kind found on denim jeans.

There are no other details in the Johnsons archives about these women, but it appears that the first was Miss Elizabeth Thompson, a blacksmith's daughter who was born in Great Yarmouth in 1869. Elizabeth lived at no. 1 Admiralty Road with her parents Charles and Elizabeth, and her siblings. In the 1901 census Elizabeth described her profession as tailoress. In the same street at the time lived Henry Gay, aged 57, an Oil Clothing Foreman, George Colby, 25, an Oil Clothing maker, Harriet George, 21, a hosiery knitting machinist, and Florence Holliday, 21, a Stocking machinist – presumably all working for Johnson & Sons. On the night of the 1911 census Elizabeth was in Leyton, Essex, visiting her aunt and uncle, but here she did declare her profession as Forewoman for a clothier's firm. After that, we can only find that her parents died and Elizabeth never married – it was a rule at Johnson's that supervisors could not keep their job if they married or had children.

Elizabeth died a spinster in Great Yarmouth hospital in October 1939. Her estate was valued at over £408, a handsome sum for a single woman at that time.[6]

Miss Watson was Margaret Hall Watson, born in 1866 the daughter of Zachariah Watson, a sawyer, and his wife Mary Ann (nee Hall), a school mistress from Lancashire. At first the couple lived in Lancashire after their marriage but moved back to Zachariah's home town of Great Yarmouth in the 1860s and settled in Row 131. Mary Ann died in 1877 at the age of 45 and it seems that Zachariah took no further part in raising his daughters: in 1881 he and his young son were visiting relations in Yorkshire while Margaret, then aged 14, had gone to live with her elder sister Sarah at George Street. At the time Margaret was described in the census as a general servant but she then found work as a machinist at Johnson's, and in the next census she was lodging in Blackfriars Road with a colleague, Selina Traxton. Neither woman has been found in the 1901 census but ten years later they were sharing a house in North Market Road and Margaret was now a forewoman at the 'oilskin clothing manufacturers.'

True to the requirements of her role, Margaret did not marry. She died in Great Yarmouth in 1945 and Selina, who also remained unmarried, moved to Worthing in Sussex where she died in 1955.

At the Johnsons' factory in Great Yarmouth, young Bridget Paston was a forewoman. She lived across the river in Gorleston, where she met her future husband Herbert 'Slasher' Watts, a barber who conveniently lived next door. (His nickname was not derogatory.)

The pair married in November 1893 and this meant that Bridget had to leave her job, but her service was recognised with a signed certificate that paid tribute to her eleven years of hard work, having started at the firm when she was 15 years old.

---

[6] National Probate Calendar (index of Wills and Administration) 1858-1966. Probate dated 11 Nov 1939

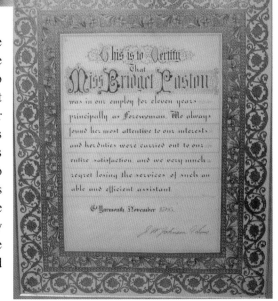

Bridget Paston and the certificate of her loyal service which reads, 'This is to Certify that Miss Bridget Paston was in our employ for eleven years principally as forewoman. We always found her most attentive to our interests and her duties were carried out to our entire satisfaction and we very much regret losing the services of such an able and efficient assistant.'

The earliest existing catalogue dates back to 1905 and illustrates the wide range of products now being made by Johnson & Sons Ltd. It also lists a Glasgow Office at 72 Great Clyde Street, in the old fish market by the docks.

Waterproofs and other protective garments for fishermen and sailing folk were still the core items in the Johnsons' business but now the two-page index also included carpenters' aprons, engineers' trousers, plasterers' jackets, butchers' coats, painters' coats and for sportsmen, football knickers, golf hose, cricket and tennis shirts and umpires' coats.

They were developing their own brand names: in 1905 they had registered the trade mark 'Wolsey' for a brand of woollen underwear guaranteed not to shrink when washed. With a hint of rather irreverent humour, they chose the Cardinal as their logo.

Following pages: illustrations from the 1905 catalogue

23

CARPENTER'S DIVIDED APRON.

BOILER SUIT.

BUTCHER'S COAT.

PAINTER'S SUIT—C15.

YACHTSMEN'S NAVY JERSEY.

Marking 2d. per letter.   Special quotations for quantities.

CHEF'S SUIT.

STEWARD'S SUIT.

DUNGAREE SUIT.

There was a serious side to the Johnson's willingness to produce woollen garments to the specification of their customers. It had long been a tradition that fishermen's pullovers were knitted with different patterns on the front: each port or fishing village had its own identifiable variation. This meant that if a man drowned at sea and his body was recovered even after days or weeks, his place of origin could be determined by the jumper he was wearing. Johnson & Sons could produce the means for such men to be brought home for burial.

The "Shamrock."

The next available document is a price list from 1913 which gives additional addresses at 15 & 16 Aldermanbury in London and 11 Cité Trévise in Paris.

The first was run by a Mr H.A. Corbett and the second by Mr J. Kleineh. Significantly, neither of these addresses is adjacent to a port, for the Johnsons were setting up central offices from which their agents could promote their ever expanding range of goods.

In this brief document, the illustration shows a rather suave-looking man modelling waterproof garments while holding a cigar.

"YARMOUTH" OILSKINS.

No. **A.6.**
The "NORFOLK" PATENT COAT double through, excellent Coat for Yachting and Boating.
12

The full catalogue for 1913 contained blue-framed pages and superior illustrations with models posed in a variety of settings.

"YARMOUTH" OILSKINS.

No. **A.10.**
The "CHAMPION" Real Silk Coat, made in various colours.
16

YARMOUTH
SOLD THROUGHOUT THE WORLD
OILSKINS

No. **A.12.**
LADIES' "F.F." COAT, made in Silk or Cambric.

No. **A.13.**
MOTORMEN'S DUCK COAT, with Special Leather Sleeves.

No. **A.19.**
REGULATION POST OFFICE CAPE.

In the same year Johnson & Sons produced a 'special shipping list' with a selection of their goods, which named their representatives in South Africa and also Australia. Their sales representatives in Britain were giving away copies of a pocket-sized reckoner containing tables of calculations which allowed retailers to work out how much profit they could make on their stock.

In the Special Autumn edition of *Men's Wear* magazine published in July 1913 an article about the men's clothing trade in Yarmouth featured the activities of Messrs Johnson & Sons Ltd. [7] It stated that almost 1,000 people were being employed by the firm and that the company had agents in France, Central America, Canada, South Africa, Australia and New Zealand. Johnson's had secured contracts with the Admiralty, the War Office, London County Council, the Metropolitan Water Board and most of the leading railway companies.

The article says, 'when our representative paid a visit to the works one of the orders in hand was for several thousand waterproof coats for the Navy made of Rexine, a new material that possesses manifold advantages as a rain-resister. Powerful band knives are constantly engaged cutting out thousands of garments of all kinds, for all climes, manufactured by this firm, and in addition to rows and rows of benches fitted with Singer sewing machines, all power-driven, manipulated by young women, in a series of well lighted and airy workrooms, there are many more engaged tending remarkable machines that produce with almost human ingenuity guernseys, stockings, mittens, and other woollen goods which it was customary to make laboriously at one time by hand alone.'

Rexine was an imitation leather material used for covering books but also used for upholstery in cars, buses and household furniture. It was manufactured by applying several coats of cellulose nitrate to cotton cloth, each layer being dried before the next was applied. Powdered pigments were mixed with oils to provide colour, and the material was engraved with heavy rollers to produce the leather-like grain.

The article relates that there were factories in Middlegate Street, at South Denes and in Gorleston, and a large building, formerly known as the Friendly Societies Hall, had been taken on for packing the goods. The journalist had just seen a number of 'stout wooden cases' leaving for South Africa.

---

[7] *Men's Wear* vol XLVI no 598 pp 91 & 113

The photo accompanying the 1913 article is captioned 'A Group of Men all wearing Yarmouth Oilskins manufactured by Messrs Johnson & Sons Ltd.' Some of the young men pictured would be leaving their jobs the following year to fight for their country in France.

Everything would change the following year with the advent of war. It is known that one employee, a young man named Ernest Gooda who was employed as a cutter, joined the Northumberland Fusiliers in 1914 and was killed in action at the Somme in October 1917. He had been home on leave the previous month, and had held his baby daughter briefly before returning to the Front. Ernest's father and three of his sisters also worked at Johnson & Sons. (See pages 52-54.)

The 1913 article had said 'The firm's relations with their army of employees are of the happiest character' and this would be a feature of Johnson & Sons for years to come. Successive bosses would appreciate that good staff relations led to loyalty and productivity: it made sound business sense, and it created a pleasant, friendly atmosphere in the workplace. The following photos were taken around this time.

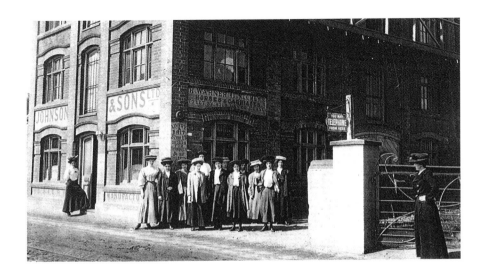

The directors at Johnson's encouraged their staff to make penny donations to Yarmouth Hospital, and the 1913 article noted that over £700 had been given in the past five years. This was a reflection of the philanthropic and community-minded nature of the Johnson family.

John William Budds Johnson had been mayor of the town in 1899 and was elected Alderman. He was a staunch Conservative and a high-ranking member of the Freemasons. In 1885 he had welcomed H.R.H. Prince Albert Victor of Wales to a meeting, and would have held the Prince's arm during proceedings. At this time Prince Albert was expected to succeed to the throne after his father Edward, but he died in a flu epidemic seven years later and it was his brother George who would become King.

John and his wife Eliza had eight children and lived for many years in Camperdown Road, Great Yarmouth, in an imposing three-storey terraced house near to the sea. Towards the end of his life he lived at Hill House at Hethersett near Norwich; he suffered several years of ill health before passing away there in 1908, and the flags at Great Yarmouth Town Hall were flown at half mast as a mark of respect.

Right: John William Budds Johnson in Mason's robes

Arthur Herbert was now the last of his generation, but he still had a few years left in which to take the family firm forward, and his energy and commitment was felt throughout the town.

Arthur had become a wealthy man and had moved house several times, increasing his living space and the number of domestic staff as he went. By 1901 he had made his final move to 23 Euston Road, Great Yarmouth – this impressive house near the seafront is now a care home with rooms for 25 residents.

Arthur's wife Charlotte, nicknamed Nellie, had borne him eight children, six of whom survived, and the couple had enjoyed the fruits of his long hours both at the factory and office, and in public life. She had had the help of nursemaids to raise her family and servants to cook and clean. It seems that the couple did not send their children away to school as many middle class parents tended to do.

The pair had married in June 1873; Charlotte, nee Muffett, had been born in Swaffham, the daughter of a carpenter and a shopkeeper. Twenty five years later Arthur and Charlotte, or 'Nellie' as she was known, celebrated their silver wedding anniversary and shared their good fortune with around 600 men and women who were employed by the firm. A newspaper report of the festivities explained that half of the girls - about 230 of them - were entertained on one evening at Winton's Assembly Rooms, and the rest, about 200, a few days later. In between these events approximately 150 male staff had dinner at the Minor Hall of the Royal Aquarium, and a menu from that day shows the feast to have included roast beef, mutton, veal and ham, with boiled beef and carrots and boiled lamb. There were sweets of hot plum pudding, fruit tarts, blancmange and wine jelly followed by bread, cheese, celery and plenty of ale.

The newspaper journalist commented that as the guests fell upon 'the good things which a legion of waiters plied them with, a merrier, jollier company you could not have imagined. Perhaps they catch it from their well-liked managing director, whose *bon homie* is proverbial but it is a well-known fact that genial sociable qualities are inherent in a gathering of Johnson's employees. They possess the virtue of setting out with the determination of enjoying themselves, and do so to the last dreg and in such a manner that others, though only temporarily associated with them, can also enjoy to the top of their bent.'

After the meal there were songs and recitations, many performed by employees, and a toast to the health of the couple was proposed by George Cross, the oldest employee who had worked for the firm for 32 years and Mr W. Howard, who had 31 years' service; neither men accustomed to speech-making, they were helped by foreman Henry Gay. Henry paid tribute to the couple and mentioned the 'true hearted friendship' that existed between employer and employee at Johnson's. He said that a few weeks earlier 'Mr Arthur' had said that he did not always aim to make the most money, but to employ the most labour.

To that end, said Henry, their managing director 'was launching out into every branch of manufacture, and he hoped the day would not be far distant when Johnson & Sons Ltd would be the largest employers of labour in the district.' This ambition was met with hearty cheers.

When Arthur rose to thank them all for their good wishes he too turned attention to the business and remarked that twenty five years ago the company had not been so large, but he hoped that in another twenty five years it would be double the size, and that many sons of those men present would also be working for them then. He said that when he had been apprenticed himself he had worked from seven in the morning to ten at night, but he had made sure that the hours his employees worked were 51 to 53 a week, less than the unions in the North were striving to achieve. He said he felt that the workers were just as productive, because he and his brother went among them and took an interest – if anyone had a problem, they could come to him.

Finally Arthur said that marriage was the best thing in the world, and that those who were not married, ought to be. He said the next best thing was good health, which he had also been blessed with. Unfortunately, his brother John William Budds Johnson was already ill at that time and could not attend, but a toast to his health was made.

Arthur's aims for developing Johnson & Sons Ltd had been made clear, but he also had vast reserves of time and energy for public work. Politically he was independent but he served on the town council for 17 years and was made an Alderman. He was chairman of the Electricity and the Distress Committees; as a member of the Education Committee he had been manager of two schools and visited them when he could, and he served on other groups including the Juvenile Employment Committee. He had spoken out against 'irregularities' in local elections, and although he was made a magistrate he did not have enough time to make many appearances at the Bench. It was said of him that 'no good cause ever made appeal to him in vain,' and later it was revealed that he had privately helped many a worker who was getting married or had suffered ill health or a bereavement.

Charlotte Johnson died in 1905 and Arthur continued to work tirelessly for the family firm alongside his sons, and to contribute to the local community life. In 1907 he welcomed the Archbishop of Canterbury Dr Randall Davidson to stay at his home during the Church Congress held in the town that year. In 1911 a fishing boat was named after him: the steam drifter 'Arthur H Johnson' built by Messrs Beeching of Yarmouth. The firm was owned by his son's father-in-law.

Even Arthur could not go on forever and he passed away after a short illness in October 1917. The funeral was held at St Nicholas church, and the attendance was such that the church was full and people lined the approach road three or four deep to see the procession arrive. The coffin was carried by long-serving employees and although the family had asked for no floral tributes, many were sent.

Several memorials to Arthur Herbert Johnson were established: the newly renovated hall at St Peter's church was dedicated to him, and later an impressive reredos or carved oak screen was commissioned in his memory (now in St Mary's church, Southtown.) Johnson's employees made a collection of over £250 which was sent to Great Yarmouth Hospital to pay for a bed in his memory.

By this time Britain had seen a great deal of injury and suffering during the course of the First World War. The company was now in the capable hands of Arthur's sons Frank, Edwin and Oswald, and it would be they who were tasked with carrying forward the work and reputation of J. W. Johnson & Sons Ltd.

Pictured in 1900 at the wedding of Edith Johnson, (left to right): Edwin and Frank Johnson, the groom Trenham Cresswell, Harold and Oswald Johnson

Chapter Three

The material world

It appears that Johnson & Sons Ltd continued to operate at full capacity during the period 1914 -18 and, as they were producing vital protective clothing for seamen in particular, it is likely that their male staff were exempt from call-up; although some may have felt it their duty to go off to war. Women workers were taking on many roles previously reserved for men in peacetime and this may have affected the ability of Johnson's to recruit new machinists. However inventories of the factories and their machines suggest that investment in new equipment and repairs were as brisk as ever, and it is assumed that there was sufficient staff to keep them operating.

Among the countless floral tributes at the funeral of Arthur Johnson in October 1917 there were contributions from 'Girls in Miss Watson's Room', 'Girls in Miss Thompson's Room', 'Girls in Miss Cubitt's Room' and 'Girls in Miss Hudson's Room', as well as a tribute labelled 'In Loving Remembrance' from the four forewomen themselves.

The first two ladies have been mentioned in chapter two. Miss Cubitt was Anna Maria, born in Great Yarmouth in 1870. Her father Samuel was a boat builder and was earning enough to employ a servant when his children were young. In the 1911 census he and his wife were living in Isaac's Road, Cobholm with their 46 year old daughter Emily helping at home and Annie was living there too – she recorded her occupation as Manageress, Johnson's – Fishermen's Outfitter. A boarder in the house was Gertrude Greasley, recorded as a forewoman at Johnson's; she had come from Leicestershire where she had been working as a hosiery machinist. It is likely that Annie remained working at Johnson's virtually until her death in 1933 at the age of 63: in those days employees could continue for as long as they were fit and able.

Miss Hudson was Beatrice Lily, born in Helhoughton near Fakenham in 1879, where her father John was a shepherd at Hubbard Farm. He died before Beatrice was 12 years old and her mother was left to raise her seven children alone. She became a laundress, but soon after Beatrice found work as a machinist at Johnson's factory in Gorleston and moved to the town to live with her widowed aunt. In 1915 Beatrice's aunt died, but Beatrice did not remain alone for long. Four years later she married Leonard Plume, a blacksmith who had been away fighting in France, and they moved back to her home area near Fakenham. Beatrice was not a young bride, but in 1922 at the age of 43 she gave birth to a daughter whom the couple named Irene. Beatrice died in 1946.

Beatrice had been more fortunate than many of her colleagues: several former Johnson's employees recalled that when they joined the firm in later years there were a number of elderly spinsters who stayed until they could no longer work: most of these women had never married because their fiancés were killed during the First World War.

There are clues to the effects the war was having on trade at Johnson & Sons Ltd: on a price list for 1917 there is no longer any mention of a representative in Australia – exports may have been curtailed – but more pointedly a note on the front cover of the document states 'During the war, all quotations, contracts and delivery promises are subject to cancellation and are accepted without engagement or responsibility, and prices are subject to alteration with or without notice.'

Prices had already increased by up to 30% on some items since 1913, and the range in this simple four page leaflet was much reduced. There were still a few lightweight outfits which had previously been promoted as suitable for yachting, but the emphasis was on the basic, durable oilskins. Without doubt they would have continued working on Government contracts throughout this time.

When the war was over, Johnson & Sons were quick to look for new markets and their catalogue for 1921, aimed at the export trade, highlights their range of 'Working Attire and Trade Clothing' including hygienic overalls for those handling food, protective clothing for mechanics, and 'native wear' for those employed in the Colonies. It adds, 'The great development of Motoring has created new channels, both of business and pastime, in which special clothing is necessary.'

Left: The Brooke motoring smock from 1913 catalogue

They were importing and using large quantities of cotton fabric and their factory at Gorleston specialised in all kinds of shirts from 'fancy cambric' to flannelette and tweed, as well as pyjamas and overalls. In 1929 Johnson & Sons Ltd exhibited their garments at The British Industries Fair in Birmingham. As well as oilskin clothing made under the registered brand name Yarmouth Oilskins they exhibited Rexine waterproof coats, woollen jerseys, cardigans and hosiery, and now they had two new lines to promote: 'Monument' shirts and pyjamas, and 'Holdfast' cotton clothing.[8] The logo for the first depicted the Great

---

[8] www.gracesguide.co.uk/Johnson_and_Sons

Yarmouth Britannia monument dedicated to Admiral Nelson, and for the second a whimsical illustration showing two bears trying to pull a pair of trousers apart was accompanied by the promise 'bears any strain.'

At this time Frank Johnson, son of Arthur Herbert, was a director and it seems he had a particular knowledge of and interest in the value of good publicity. He had business interests not only in the family firm and in Yarmouth Stores Ltd but also in the Yare Printing Company in King Street, which now had the contract for publishing Johnson's catalogues. These had previously been produced by Frederick Mann of Howard Street. The new editions would introduce full colour illustrations.

In an interview with a reporter from the *Great Yarmouth Mercury* in June 1930 Frank talked about his roles on various committees of the local council, and in particular as Chairman of the Piers Committee. Asked about how he would suggest the town might increase the revenue of the Wellington Pier and Gardens he advocated a longer tourist season adding, 'I should be in favour of spending more on advertising... Advertising benefits all, though you do not directly see it.'

The article described Frank's character as one of courtesy and consideration for the feelings of others. It said, 'He enjoys the advantage of bearing a name held in peculiar honour throughout the town,' adding that his father Arthur had 'bequeathed him a great ideal of public service and of big hearted sympathy for his fellow men...' The municipal arena was enriched, it said, 'by his quiet efficiency and modest nature.'

Throughout the years when the Johnson family were directly involved in the business, their associates and employees would pay tribute to the considerate and fair minded character of the men folk. It was this mutual respect that helped make the Johnsons' factories such agreeable places to work.

Frank's wish to see more tourists brought to the seaside town came true in the mid 1930s, with large-scale improvements to the Golden Mile. The fishing industry was booming too: a lucrative deal with Russia had encouraged a local businessman to erect a new cold store for smoked herring, bringing the promise of long-term jobs – and trade for Johnson's and Yarmouth Stores too, supplying the fishermen and the ancillary workers.[9]

Frank Johnson

---

[9] Article by "Peggotty" in *Great Yarmouth Mercury* 12th November 2010

However, work out of season was scarce and local unemployment was high. In a later article former Johnson's machinist Emmie Mitchell told a journalist that between the wars there was little choice of career for most women in Great Yarmouth, it was either domestic service or factory work. She had started at the Admiralty Road oilskin factory in 1925 when she was 15 and, she said, 'It could be extremely hard work, depending on the orders we got. The busiest time was during the winter, when we would sometimes get a large order from Norwegian fishermen.'

She continued, 'During the summer there was less to do; but our boss, Frank Johnson, would always try to find us work elsewhere if there was nothing that needed to be done in his factory. He often got us employment on the town's tea stalls. He was a very considerate man.'[10]

Some young men managed to get work at Johnson & Sons: one example was Bert 'Sailor' Brown who had left school in Gorleston in about 1930 and begun working as an apprentice sewing machine mechanic at Pier Plain. His first love was football and in his spare time he played for Gorleston F.C., which led to a contract with Charlton Athletic and a place in the postwar F.A. Cup Final. He returned to Gorleston as player-manager and coach, retiring in 1956, having become a local legend among sports fans. 'Sailor' died in 2009 at the age of 93.[11]

The Johnson family were to lose a valued member in May 1934 when William James, son of John William Budds Johnson, passed away at the age of 61. 'Mr Willie' as he was called had been a director of Johnson & Sons Ltd as well as a director and secretary of Yarmouth Stores Ltd. He had held shares in the Norfolk and Suffolk Brick Company, he was a member of two local Conservative clubs and had also been a town councillor, but according to his obituary, 'Public life did not greatly appeal to his genial, unassuming personality, and his happiest moments were spent with his family.'

---

[10] *Great Yarmouth Mercury* 3 November 1989 p14
[11] *Eastern Daily Press* 22 January 2009

44

William's funeral took place at Ormesby where he had spent his boyhood, but with the factories closed for the morning many Johnson's employees made the journey to attend, and six of them carried his coffin. A list of mourners published in the newspaper included those from two of the departments, and it is worth reproducing below, as there are no other staff records for that period in existence.

The men who carried the coffin were: J. Angel, T. Collett, Harry Halfnight, E. Hipgrave, R.G. Manthorpe and H. Turrell.

Men who attended from the Admiralty Road oilskin department were: A. Larman (manager) C. Reynolds, G. Hodds, H.A. Bracey, W.R. Burgell, A. Barber, J. Barber, H. George, W. Stearn, C.W. Davey, W. Storey, H. Howard, E.F. Newman, S. Bream, F. Sivell, J.J. Bradnum, Bertie Brackenbury, J. Clements, A.G. King, P. James, A.C. Moore, R. Page, W. Burley, B. Dean, R. Ringwood, and R. Jarrad.

Women members of the oilskin department are not listed except for forewomen Miss Denmark and Miss Sparks.

From the Middlegate Street factory the male staff members were: E.B. Ward (cashier), B. Provart, W. Parker, H. Bloomfield, T. Burgess, H.J. Palmer, S.D. Halfnight, C. Sharman, S.J. Aldous, G.L. Flatford, H. Hellenburgh, and W. Overill. Forewomen Misses Watson, Thompson, Crowe and Magnus are mentioned.

Probate was later granted to Emily, William's widow, and to his son William Dudley, whose occupation was given as Manufacturing Outfitter. Although Dudley, as he was known, did enter the business it appears that he did not take a prominent role. William's brother Jack was also involved in the firm. In 1907 he married Hilda Dove, the daughter of mill owner Frank Dove, bringing together two prosperous Yarmouth families. The couple lived at Ormesby and had two daughters and a son, who did not enter the business.

It would be the sons of Arthur Herbert: Frank, Edwin and Oswald, and their sons, who would take the company forward. To publicise their goods and give credit to their hardworking staff, the following pictures were taken in the Yarmouth and Gorleston factories in the early 1930s.

Above and below: machinists at Pier Plain, Gorleston

Above: Gorleston shirt room. Below: cutting room at Great Yarmouth

In 1935 there was a major change in the Johnsons' business interests: William Knights, vice chairman and managing director of the Yarmouth Stores Ltd, offered to buy out the Johnsons from the company. He purchased all the holdings of Frank, Edwin and Oswald which automatically disqualified them as directors and, with his wife Emma, his son William Robert Mobbs Knights and daughter-in-law Nelly, William took control of the company. Only a few shares remained in the hands of outsiders including two members of the Johnson family, but consensus among the Knights partners was enough to carry any vote.

The Johnsons could once again concentrate on manufacturing, while the Yarmouth Stores Ltd remained one of their major customers. However the relationship would not run smoothly for long. Until now there had been restrictions on Yarmouth Stores and their ability to buy from anyone other than Johnson's; records show that permission had to be given before they could source stock elsewhere. One of William Knights's plans for the firm was to open a wholesale department and to produce their own line of shirts and overalls at a factory near the main store in South Quay, in competition with his former partners. Naturally this would cause some acrimony between the two families in the coming years.

Meanwhile Edwin, whose wife Gertrude had died in May 1935, married again a few months later: his new bride was Laura Elvina Augusta Westgate, the daughter of a market gardener and 21 years younger than Edwin.

Edwin and Laura Johnson

Great change was coming, not only to the firm of Johnson & Sons Ltd, but to Great Yarmouth itself – the 1930s saw the start of wide scale clearance of the old Rows which had been condemned as slums. Enemy military action would take over this work of destruction, because of course great change was coming to the whole country and its people. In a rather chilling sign of foreboding, the Johnson's catalogue for October 1936 had carried the following note inside the front cover:

Air Raid Precautions :

● ●

It is stated officially that the best material for resisting the penetration of **Liquid Mustard Gas** is **OILSKIN** of the type used in the Navy.

MESSRS. JOHNSON & SONS, LIMITED, Great Yarmouth, are Manufacturers of complete **PROTECTIVE SUITS OF OILSKIN** of this description, which they supply to various Government Departments, and they will be pleased to supply particulars on application.

Chapter Four

Wartime by the Sea

There are former members of staff who still vividly remember life at the Johnson's factories before the war. Olive Davies, nee Browne, worked at the Admiralty Road oilskins factory. The fishing industry was in her blood: Olive recalls, 'My mother was a Scots fisher girl from Wick, she met my father here – he was a Yarmouth man. She was Maggie Manson, they used to come down to do the herring. Our family ate a lot of fish – we practically lived on fish.'

Olive was born in 1920 and started working at Johnson's at the age of 14. She said, 'I was a "runabout" first, doing odd jobs, and then they put me on sewing buttons on, all day long. And then they started me on oilskins – doing the hats – what the fishermen used to wear, sou'westers. I went on the sewing machine, there was loads of machines all going at once.'

The oilskin material was heavy and greasy to handle. Olive says she wore an apron to cover her clothes from neck to foot. Another employee at the factory had been Herbert 'Bertie' Brackenbury, whose granddaughter Monica Barber remembers that when he came home his trousers were dark and shiny with the oil from the fabric. 'He didn't have overalls,' she explains, 'just ordinary trousers. They were shiny all the way down and you could smell the oil on them. I don't suppose he could wash them, of course, with that oil on them.'

According to former chief mechanic Ronnie Webb, oilskin workers' trousers 'could almost stand up on their own' and would give off an even stronger smell when warm – later he introduced a uniform white coat for protection.

Monica's aunt, the late Sheila Tate, also worked at the Admiralty Road factory, overcoming the fact that she had sight only in her right eye. Sheila went to live with Monica for a while and used to cycle from Caister to the Admiralty Road factory every day.

Left: Sheila Tate.
Below: machining oilskins

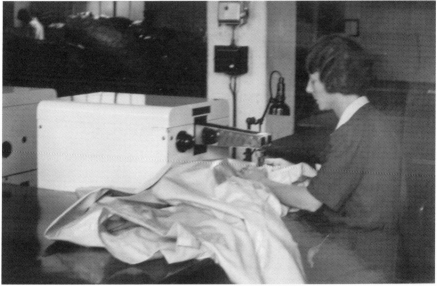

At Pier Plain, Gorleston, Vera Mallion nee Beavers started work in the year before war broke out. She recalls, 'Those were the days when you finished school at 14 on the Friday and on the Monday you were at work. I went to Johnson's and saw Miss Gooda, and she said "Yes you can start – what would you like to do, would you like to learn the sewing machine?" I said I didn't really mind. I started off as a runabout. If the girls on the machines wanted a mechanic or anything, they'd call you because they didn't want to leave their machines – they were on piece work. After a while I got on a machine and before long I was finishing a whole shirt '

Miss Gooda was from a large family living in Great Yarmouth – it was not an uncommon name in the town – and her father Charles had taken his family to Yorkshire for a while, where he worked as a porter at Beverely Union Workhouse. They had returned to Yarmouth by 1890 and Charles worked at Johnson's in the oilskin factory where he was later described as a kind man who never thought ill of anybody, and was 'never known to do an unkind thing or speak an angry word.' He continued to work for the firm until he was 72.

The Gooda family, about 1908. Left to right rear: Florence, Alice, Charles, Ethel, Gertie. Centre: George, Charles, Eva, Elizabeth, Grace. Front: Ernest

There were nine children in the family, only three of them boys, and sadly Charles junior died in 1912 of pneumonia, possibly associated with T.B. Another son, Ernest, who had worked at Johnson's in the cutting room, died at the Somme in 1917. (See page 31.) The last, George, went away to London to work in a wholesale drapery warehouse, which may have been connected with Johnson's.

Of the daughters, three did not marry and they all worked at Johnson's. It was the eldest, Florence, who was forewoman at the Pier Plain factory. She had been born in 1878 while her father was employed at the workhouse in Yorkshire but after the family came back to Yarmouth she and her sisters Gertrude and Alice found jobs as machinists at Johnson's. At first they were living with their parents in Exmouth Road, Great Yarmouth, but later the women lived comfortably in Springfield Road, Gorleston. By now Alice had stopped work in order to keep house but Florence and Gertie used to catch the rowing boat ferry across the river to work at Yarmouth, until Florence became a supervisor at Pier Plain which was within walking distance of her home.

The three ladies are remembered by younger relations and work colleagues as being 'real Victorian' – they dressed sombrely in long grey or navy dresses with lace trimmings, and tended to wear their hair tied back in a bun. One niece who used to visit them at Springfield Road remembers having tea with homemade shortbread served on delicate china and lace cloths, in their beautiful walled garden.

Although the Gooda sisters did have a sense of humour, and Florence is remembered as being the one with the softer nature, nevertheless the girls who worked under her never dared share a joke with her, nor talked about her home life. 'She was no gadabout', says one, referring to the reserved, serious manner of her supervisor. However, she always had a smile for their boss 'Mr Noel' when he came to the factory – his old-fashioned charm and gentlemanly manners were not lost on her.

According to former members of staff, Florence was diligent at work and even checked that any new girls had clean hands before they were allowed to touch the fabrics.

Florence and Gertrude Gooda

Florence passed away in 1964 at the age of 85, and was buried in the grave of her sister Gertrude who had died two years earlier. Alice survived another 11 years. Vera Mallion reflects, 'Miss Gooda was the sweetest person you could ever wish to meet.' Having taken the big step from school to work, Vera found that Florence Gooda was like a second mother: kind, helpful and encouraging.

Vera recalls her early impressions of the Gorleston factory as it was in 1938. 'It was a huge great place and you walked in where the girls used to smoke – a sort of tea room – then when you went in the main room all you could see was the big ironing boards with big irons, and then great big benches with all the machines on. You all had a basket each and you went up to the table where Miss Gooda sat up at the top overlooking everything. You took your book which she would write in, she would give you a bundle of pieces, sleeves and cuffs and so on, to take and put in your basket, and then you'd get started on sewing them.

Some girls worked on a conveyor belt, just doing one thing and they'd put it back on the belt for the next person. At the end the last woman would be standing, she'd do the buttons and the button holes. I learned to do that; it was better money if you were quick. I earned about ten shillings a week, and gave my mother two and six a week.'

It was a family atmosphere at Pier Plain, especially as many of the employees knew each other outside the factory. Vera was being taught by Gladys Parker whose father was lifeboat man 'Shoots' Parker, and Vera's own father was coxswain at one time. His name was Bertie 'Totie' Beavers, who worked on the pilot boat at Yarmouth Harbour for 21 years, and was a well known character in the town.

One of Vera's close colleagues was Irene Bullen, whose maiden name of Collins was also familiar locally as her father Alfred 'Shiner' Collins had been tug master and was later lighthouse keeper at the end of the pier. Her first job was to take work back to the machinists if they had made a mistake, so that they could unpick it and do it again. It was an unenviable task to be taking rejects back, as the girls were only paid for work completed satisfactorily. But Irene also remembers the happy atmosphere of the factory. 'I knew a lot of people from school, it was a nice place to work,' she says. 'They were a super lot of girls.'

Irene also comments that for girls there were few career choices; it was mainly factory work or going into service, and she didn't fancy the latter. For Irene, who lived near the factory, it was handy to work so close to home and have no fares to pay. For those who had to cross the river to go and work in Yarmouth, transport was another issue. Irene adds 'You could get the ferry across from Ferry Boat Hill – at first that had cost half a penny and later a penny. But nobody liked to use it – it was only a rowing boat. My mother worked at the Denes and she'd walk up and round rather than go on the boat, especially if the sea was rough.'

At the outbreak of war, civilian clothing soon became rationed but Johnson & Sons Ltd attracted numerous Government contracts, particularly oilskin anti-gas garments – over a million and a half items would be produced for the armed services in the coming years.

The catalogue for 1938 had displayed an array of new, patriotic brand names that made much of the company's contracts with the armed services.

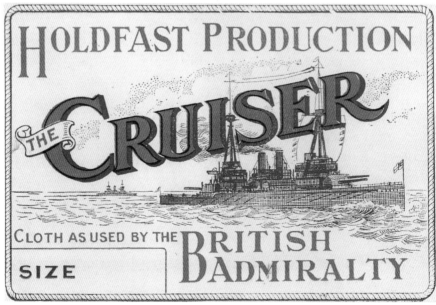

At Pier Plain, production was concentrated on shirts – three quarters of a million were ordered in total, with the same number of boiler suits and overalls required. At their hosiery factory which was now in the former Masonic building in Row 108, Johnson's were producing thousands of Guernsey sweaters and pairs of socks and mittens for the Merchant Navy and for fishermen.[12] With problems in obtaining the raw materials, the directors were also having to comply with regulations that were being issued by the Government, in particular the newly formed Ministry of Supply, which was created to oversee and co-ordinate the supply of equipment to the forces. The Ministry had control over all essential materials including leather, cotton and wool – the staples that Johnson & Sons needed for manufacturing.

A surviving handwritten document gives an insight to the firm's dealings during the years 1939-45. It states, 'This business has been established in Great Yarmouth for more than 100 years and has always produced clothing for Government Departments, Local Authorities, Fishing Trade, Mercantile Marine, essential services and export. Examples of the types of clothing supplied are:

"Yarmouth" brand oilskin clothing for fishermen, merchant navy, agricultural workers and miners.

"Monument" brand shirts – Oxfords, Harvards, Grandrilles, Khaki & Blue Drill.

"Holdfast" brand cotton protective clothing of all types (boiler suits, bib & brace, khaki coats, drill jackets & trousers)

"Monument" brand hosiery – heavy type half-hose, seamen's knitted Jerseys & Guernseys and sea boot stockings

"Monument" brand woollen clothing, seamen's clothing, (patrol suits & man o' war suits), heavy work trousers.

Pre-war exports were to Norway, Iceland, Faroe Isles, Holland, Belgium, France, Newfoundland, South America, Palestine and South Africa.

---

[12] *Great Yarmouth Mercury* 23 February 1946.

Since 1939 production has been mainly for the Government Departments and essential services. All sections of the business are under the Essential Works Order and the factories have been granted Nucleus Certificates by the Board of Trade.'

The Nucleus Certificates related to a Government concentration policy whereby smaller factories had to organise themselves into clusters which had no less than 50 employees and with no less than 75% of their clothing production being on government contracts, in order to maximise efficiency. Naturally Johnson's did not have to combine with other firms to comply on size, but they required Cloth Certificates before they could be allocated the materials. The Essential Work (General Provisions) Order was produced in March 1941 so that the Government could direct labour where it was needed most. In the case of Johnson's this would have helped them retain their staff, although of course the men – and the women too – were often keen to get away and take a more active role in the military.

Vera Mallion said, 'I left Johnson's and went into the forces – one of the girls came in to the factory wearing an air force uniform and she looked so lovely I wanted to be in the WAAF too. So four of us went straight over and joined up together. I forged my age as I was only 17 but really, if you could breathe you were in. We all ended up as balloon operators, working on the winches that made the barrage balloons go up and down. After that I was a mechanic on the aircraft, on instrument repairs and just before D-Day I painted white stripes on the wings of the Spitfires.'

However, before Vera left she had time to experience the reality of wartime in Gorleston. She said, 'Johnson's had an air raid shelter in a dugout, like an Anderson shelter, in the grounds. It was a concrete tunnel with benches either side. When the sirens went we were all down there like a shot with our sandwiches and our knitting, sewing, crochet – all that sort of thing. And then the all clear would go and we'd all get up, just get to the door and the siren would go again. One day this went on all day until it was time to go home.'

Vera says that nobody panicked, because fairly quickly everyone became used to the upheaval, and the noise of the guns and the bombs. However, being paid 'piece work' rates meant that the staff received no wages for the time when they couldn't work.

Irene Collins left too: in 1942 she joined the Wrens, hoping to be posted to HMS Watchful, the Naval barracks at Yarmouth. Instead she was sent to join the ATS at Liverpool. While on leave Irene met a Gorleston lad named Harry Bullen who was in the 11th Hussars and, she recalls, 'We met on the Monday; on Tuesday he said he would marry me and on the Wednesday he remembered to ask me!' The couple would move away from Gorleston, but Irene has remained firm friends with Vera for over 70 years.

Olive Browne wasn't allowed to join up; her mother, the former Scots herring girl, refused to allow it. Olive says, 'I was about 18 when war came. My friends went in the services and I wanted to go in but your mother had to sign to give permission. My mother said "I'm not signing it – I've got two sons in already and I'm not going to let you go." We spent a lot of time down in the air raid shelter. I played the accordion for the little children, before they all got evacuated. There was an older boy left, he was about 14 and when it was my 21st birthday he put trimmings round the shelter for me. The Blackfriars pub was over the road and I went and got some orange juice for them all. That was my 21st birthday.'

At the oilskin factory in Admiralty Road, there was no shelter specifically for the workers. Phyllis Johnson nee Newson started working there in 1940 at the age of fourteen. She said, 'I worked on the top floor of the factory and if the sirens went off we had to go to the ground floor for safety as there were no shelters.'

Phyllis started off working for forewoman Miss Denmark, who, she says, 'was a little tiny lady with grey hair. She never had much contact with you, only making your book up and giving your pay packet out. She never came round to look at what you were doing.' Phyllis's first job was to put paper in oilskin coats to protect the inner linings when they were treated and sealed. But she was keen to be a machinist and says she pestered the bosses to give her a chance.

For a time Phyllis made sou'westers, and in the photo right she is modelling one on the roof of the factory in Admiralty Road. She was still a teenager at the time, and was picked to go and pose for the photographer, while there were lookouts and soldiers with a Bofors gun stationed on the roof. No doubt there were a few comments passed between them.

Phyllis confirms that working with the oilskin material was a messy business: she says, 'When I was on oilskins I was courting then, and the oil used to get in your hair, you had to try and get the smell out as well – we didn't have showers then, you just washed it.' Her work was appreciated though, and she progressed to making samples for the firm, one day completing 12 coats in a single shift.

According to former supervisor Peggy Driver, there were 54 pieces to a coat.

After the war Phyllis would have a special outfit to make: an order was placed for waterproof garments for the Duke of Edinburgh who was going sailing with the famous if eccentric boat designer and yachtsman, Uffa Fox.

Phyllis had a secret method for speeding up her production rate, as she explains. 'The machines were driven by a belt which would stretch and after a while it slowed the machine down. We were supposed to wait to have it replaced when it broke, and the mechanic would turn the power off to do it, that stopped all the machines. But I used to go underneath and unhook the belt from the shaft while it was still moving. I'd chop a bit off and put it back together, then flip it back on again.'

It was a dangerous practice. Girls were warned against having long hair because it was all too easy to get it caught in the fast-spinning drive wheels. Another well known hazard was from the sewing machine needles: almost every girl would catch her finger at some time, and many have repeated the mantra that 'You weren't a real machinist until you'd got a needle in your finger.'

Phyllis recalls, 'Audrey Brown who sat next to me, she'd get a needle through her finger. You'd have to hold her down and turn the wheel to release her – several times she did that. She'd just go and get a plaster put on it, and carry on.'

Others were not so relaxed about it. Doreen Flower nee Wright, who worked at the Conge factory after the war, said 'The machines went so fast, it wasn't so much when the needle went in your finger - the pain came when you were getting it out. When it happened to me I had to go and lie down afterwards, I felt I was going to pass out.'

Barbara Bailey nee Robinson also worked there but managed not to actually get the needle through her finger – however when one of the other girls did, she couldn't bear to watch and used to go and hide in one of the big wicker storage baskets until the unfortunate girl had been released and treated.

Back at Admiralty Road, the staff had no thoughts about sewing machines and dangers from needles on the morning of 5th June 1941. At

3.44 a.m. a 4,000 lb bomb had been dropped over the factory but it had landed in the road and failed to go off. The area was cordoned off and the girls were turned away while bomb disposal experts made the device safe. As can be seen in the photograph below, onlookers were not kept at much of a distance.

The severity of war was more than apparent to the staff at Johnson's. Civilians were subject to machine gunning by enemy aircraft as they cycled to work, and Sheila Tate, cycling in from Caister, once had to jump off her bike and hide under trees near the Smith's Crisp factory as the bombers droned overhead.

Middlegate Street had been targeted in January; in April the German bombers completed the task and the Johnson's factory was destroyed. Phyllis Noble nee Burman had been working at the factory until then. She recalls, 'The factory in Middlegate Street was three storeys. The ground floor was for all the cutting out, the first was where they made all the khaki clothing and the top was where they used to make jackets and trousers. I had started there at 14 as a marker – lining up the buttonholes for the buttons or eyelets to go in. Then I went on a machine, hemming garments first, and then they put me on oilskins. It was heavy to work on. I made oilskins for the lifeboat men, you made them throughout – made your own buttonholes, and serge collar; they were lined throughout with yellow oilskin. We got 1/9d a garment and it took two hours to make one. So time was money.'

Phyllis adds, 'I was just turned 16 when the war broke out. I remember there was a terrible raid that night (in 1941) – incendiary bombs were dropping everywhere and when we went out the next morning the factory had gone and everything you had in it like scissors and overalls. I had no job.'

Some of the staff transferred to working at Admiralty Road, although that too had suffered bomb damage in February that year.

Bomb damage at Johnson's oilskin works, Admiralty Road.
Picture from *Great Yarmouth Frontline Town 1939-45* by Charles G Box OBE

By the time of the most intense raids, many employees had already moved inland. On instructions from the Ministry of Supply, Johnson's had transferred its hosiery works to a property in Bulwer Road, Leicester in July 1940. Previously they had been operating at the former Masonic Hall in Row 108 Great Yarmouth, but the building was destroyed by bombing the following year and production would not return there.

At the same time a building in Stockport was taken on: the former Robinsons tobacco factory in St Petersgate. A number of staff went with the company, finding lodgings in the area; the Gooda sisters were among them. Lily Read, nee Bush, had started working at Middlegate Street as a 'shanker.' She explains, 'that meant putting buttons through a hole on whatever garment was already made, and a washer and ring at the back; if you worked hard enough you made 7/6d weekly.' Lily graduated to working as a machinist and says she felt 'all grown up and out to work, set for a rosy future.' But when war came she was too young to go to Stockport and instead was evacuated with her mother to Surrey.

Phyllis Noble had been trying to carry on working in spite of the very real danger of attack. She says, 'German planes used to come over early morning, machine gunning all the seaside. You still kept riding your bike; you had to get to work. I think they were trying to shoot the people who were going to work.'

Phyllis's brother Eddie Burman was Noel Johnson's 'right hand man' and he had already moved up to Stockport where he was living with his girlfriend's mother, so Phyllis was able to join them until she was called to join up - she served as a cook in the ATS. 'At Johnson's they were making boiler suits for the Admiralty, they had a big contract for that through the war,' says Phyllis.

There still exists a large bundle of invoices from the Singer Sewing Machine Company, showing that at least 198 machines plus stools, benches, lights and ancillary equipment were bought for the new works. The purchases continued in 1941, amounting to thousands of pounds in total.

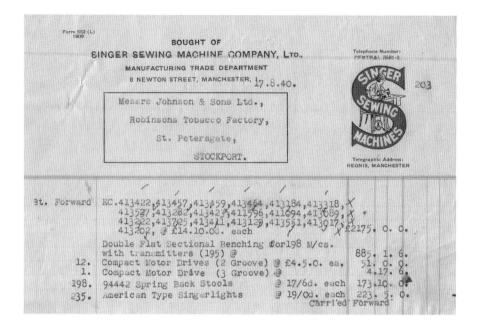

After the number and frequency of raids subsided, the Johnsons did their best to remain optimistic and keep production going. In April 1942 the firm made a large investment of over £1,014 on a new boiler for the Admiralty Road works, supplied by Dodman & Co Ltd of King's Lynn.

The workers had begun returning, first those from Leicester and soon the staff came back from Stockport too. By February 1945, before victory in Europe had actually been announced, the Johnsons were taking account of their staff and trying to predict how many would be employed post-war, and at what cost. A major problem was the fact that, having lost two buildings in Great Yarmouth completely, they were not permitted to rebuild on those sites. A table drawn on the handwritten wartime document tells the story of the devastation to the company's premises and is reproduced in appendix two.

The photo on the following page shows Johnson's staff at Vauxhall Station, ready to move to Stockport. (Photo courtesy of Chris Hopkins whose mother and aunt are right of centre.)

The prediction was that the post-war bill for wages for 570 staff would come to approximately £75,000 and that would double if they could get staff numbers back up to the pre-war total of around 1200. There was still a long struggle ahead, and no guarantee that the Johnsons could ever return their company to its earlier eminence in manufacturing.

In a moment of levity one of the women at the Admiralty Road factory penned the following rhyme, which former forewoman Peggy Driver still has in a scrapbook:

Johnson's Theme Song of the Thirties
We are but women, mild and meek,
We work for Johnson's all the week,
The more we work, the more we may,
It makes no difference to our pay.

On Monday morn we start our toil,
Among the navy serge and oil,
And on the clock our eyes are fixed,
We gently murmur "roll on six."

Above: Peggy Driver (top right) with colleagues, c.1940

Chapter Five

New Blood

While the war had been bringing all kinds of new difficulties to the home and working lives of the Johnson's employees, the Johnson family members had been fighting battles of their own both in military service and in the clothing industry. Frank, Edwin and Oswald, the sons of Arthur Herbert Johnson, had been in control of the business but they were ageing, and their own sons were being brought on board to help.

Frank had not rushed into marriage; he had wed Annie Maud Wright in 1908 when he was 33 and she was 24, and the couple had produced two sons: Russell Frank Arthur who was born in 1909 and Gordon Herbert, born in 1912. Annie died in 1923 at the age of 31 and after eight years of being widowed Frank married again, his new wife being Mabel Alice Bales.

Both of Frank's sons would enter the family business: Russell joined in 1929 and took over the oilskins factory in 1940, and Gordon, having served in the army during the war, became manager of the hosiery factory when it opened in Admiralty Road in 1946. The opening of the new premises was documented in the *Great Yarmouth Mercury* in February of that year, stating that the hosiery operation had just returned to Yarmouth after being evacuated to Leicestershire five and a half years earlier. It said that a small number of people were being employed there at first but it was hoped that the business would rapidly expand when more raw materials and skilled labour became available.

The article said, 'A reporter who was conducted over the newly acquired premises for the hosiery factory in Admiralty Road, found the factory still largely engaged on Government contracts, and socks were being turned out for the Forces, with special sea boot stockings for the

Royal Navy. Messrs Johnson & Sons are playing their part, small though it may be at the moment, in the drive general throughout the country to step up the export trade.'

The following photographs show the interior of the factory.

Elsie Thompson nee Jex started working at the hosiery factory just after the war at the age of 15. She recalls that men worked the machines on the ground floor, creating the basics of the socks and sweaters, while upstairs a team of women worked on the 'linking' machines, finishing the socks at the heel and toe, and adding the ribbing to sweaters at the neck, cuffs and waistband. The work required good eyesight, and some machines had a magnifying visor over the front.

June Finch started working at the factory in December 1951, a month before her 15th birthday. Her job was to pair up the men's woollen socks that were given to her in bundles. She said, 'they were all different sizes, you'd have a line of socks and you'd match the welts and toes to find pairs – at the end of the day you might have five or six left that didn't match.'

June stayed for five years before going to work for Birdseye because they paid much higher wages. However she remembers many of the friends she made at Johnson's and especially the dances they would sometimes hold in the factory itself, and the trips the staff would organise such as to London or to Southend-on-Sea. She was told that after she left a group of employees were encouraged to go on a sponsored walk from Yarmouth to Lowestoft, but having completed it there was no transport arranged and they had to walk back again.

June receiving a bear hug at Southend Kursaal, about 1954

June and friend Stella taking a ride on the gallopers

Above: staff from the hosiery factory

Margaret Colledge nee Skinner also worked at the hosiery factory. She said, 'They made all the big oily-wool jumpers on machines, the men did that, then the girls did the linking; that was a round machine with needles, you threaded the garment on and it did the cuffs, the necks and waistbands and the toes on socks. They were all interesting jobs.'

Margaret had started off at the oilskin factory across the road, where she did the welding on the seams of garments. She reveals one of the 'tricks of the trade' that she learned there: 'If you burnt a hole in the fabric you put in what you called "mouse turds." That was a little roll of sticky stuff, you put it in the hole and sealed it, and it formed a patch.'

The reporter who visited the factories in 1946 was told that there were plenty of orders for oilskins from many different countries, but the firm could not obtain enough raw materials to cope with them. He wrote,

'The firm is the largest manufacturer of oilskins in England, and orders include demands for 100,000 oilskin garments, some of which are from South Africa, Iceland, the Farnes and Newfoundland. The total value of the orders in the three factories runs to several hundred thousand pounds.'

There was good news at Gorleston too: the article revealed that the factory at Pier Plain was now being doubled in size and was equipped with the most up-to-date machinery, capable of turning out thousands of garments a week, but there was a shortage of female labour available. The plan was to increase wages to try to attract more staff.[13]

Frank Johnson's brother Edwin had also brought two sons into the business. In 1902 he had married Gertude Beeching, whose father Thomas was a partner in the firm that later built the steam drifter named Arthur H. Johnson. The couple had six children including two older boys, one who became a physician and the other who qualified as a chartered accountant, and it was the two younger sons, Michael and Noel, who joined the Johnson's company.

Edwin was Chairman of Johnson & Sons Ltd at this time and like the other directors had become wealthy during the years of good trading. He had been able to buy Flixton House from the Somerleyton Estate in 1919 and his children had grown up there, enjoying the extensive grounds which enabled them to take up shooting, and fishing and boating on its private lake. Michael, born in 1917, had joined the Suffolk Yeomanry before the Second World War, and had risen to the rank of major. He went to sea during the war as an anti-aircraft gunner on board armed merchant ships, but in peacetime he was a keen sailor and at one time he was Commodore of the Royal Norfolk and Suffolk Yacht Club.

Michael was a director of the firm and manager of the Gorleston shirt factory. He was careful about his own appearance: one former employee recalls that he was one of the first men the girls knew who wore cologne; they would comment to each other about the pleasant

---

[13] *Great Yarmouth Mercury* 23 February 1946

waft of fragrance as he passed by. Michael married late: in 1959 he wed divorcee Sylvia Colpus in Hove, Sussex when he was aged 42 and she was 15 years older. He worked hard at the business but his keenest interests lay beyond the factory, and in 1961 it was while sailing his yacht Hydra in a race near Lowestoft that he suffered a fatal heart attack. He passed away at the age of 44.

John Noel Johnson, always known as Noel, was born in 1923. He was only twelve years old when his mother Gertrude died and his father re-married, but he appears to have developed a good relationship with his new step-mother.

He was educated at a public school and was placed in classes above his year group because of his outstanding academic ability. He was naturally left-handed but as was common in those days he was made to write with his right, which resulted in him always having virtually illegible handwriting. Nevertheless he went on to gain an honours degree in Modern Languages at Cambridge having worked hard at his studies, but two of his greatest qualities seem to have been innate: he had a 'photographic' memory and a seemingly endless capacity for caring about his fellow men and women. His cousin David was witness to the first attribute. On one occasion he was present when an employee showed Noel an idea that he had written out in a document and it seemed as if Noel simply gave it a cursory glance. The man was outspoken in his anger at the perceived slight, but Noel was able to repeat to him exactly what had been written down and to prove that he had read and understood every word. 'Noel was the brightest of us all,' David said. 'He was the brains of the family and the firm. He had his own ideas of things and he had this charm about him, he could get what he wanted.'

Examples of Noel's caring nature are too numerous to mention but range from testimonies from countless employees who found him charming, attentive and sympathetic, to reminiscences about and tributes to his work on behalf of local hospitals, the community at large as chairman of Lowestoft Magistrates and Great Yarmouth Tax Commissioners, and even his favourite golf club at Aldeburgh where, during his time as Captain, he would greet members and make sure that they were happy with the facilities and their experiences at the club. Of course, in addition to all of this he also worked long and hard in the family firm.

Noel had joined the Royal Devon Yeomanry Artillery, reaching the rank of Acting Captain, but had been invalided out of the army in February 1944 following a motorcycle accident that put him in hospital for several months and left him with a severely damaged leg. He was a tall man, and due to his disability he required specially made shoes, and he walked with a pronounced limp. Even so he would walk around the factories, speaking to staff and enquiring about their work, their health, even their wedding plans – he never failed to notice if a special event was coming up. His daughter Susan confirms, 'My father wasn't a great one for controlling things from an office.' Members of staff recall that he was always ready to help and advise where he could.

Former machinist Joy Hawkins nee Leggett said, 'He was the first man that I know of who let us do flexi hours. I used to take my children to school, go to work, leave off and pick them up. He let people have summer holidays off too. He was a brilliant leader and he did a lot of young mums the world of good, and they were loyal to him – they worked very, very hard.'

Joy had been born in Yarmouth but was evacuated in 1940 and did not see her mother again for three years. While she was away the family home was partially destroyed in the bombing and eventually they moved to Gorleston. Joy said, 'I came back to Pier Walk on the Friday and in the afternoon my mother took my sister and me to Johnson's. We started on the Monday. Nobody had a lot of choice where you worked – your money helped to feed the family. My mother had sixteen children, fourteen surviving.'

Apart from time away in the A.T.S. and when Joy was first married and had her children, she worked at Pier Plain, Gorleston. Noel and the management team were by now based in a brand new factory with offices which they had built on the corner of the Conge and North

Quay in Great Yarmouth (staff tended to refer to this factory as 'The Conge'). The firm had bought the land on a long lease and building work began in October 1947, after lengthy negotiations with the local authorities. An article in the *Eastern Evening News* stated, 'The actual manufacturing, which will employ between 150 and 200 women, will begin as soon as adequate machinery becomes available, and will do much to relieve the daily journeys of some 80-100 girls between Yarmouth and the firm's Gorleston branch, which will continue with exclusively Gorleston labour.'

The newspaper stated that the building would be expanded until it could accommodate 400 employees and there were plans to enlarge it further over the course of the next 20 years.[14]

The Johnson's factory on the corner of the Conge and North Quay

---

[14] *Eastern Evening News* 8 January 1948

That year, 1947, had started out less auspiciously with the worst winter on record, and snow falling so heavily that coal supplies were frozen in at depots and roads blocked. Without enough fuel reaching the power stations, the government reacted by restricting domestic electricity supplies and enforcing power cuts to industry. In February Johnson & Sons had to close the factories for over a fortnight. Ironically, they had previously been reliant on steam to power the machines and possibly could have coped if they had had enough stocks of coke to keep them running. But they had changed over to electricity and were at the mercy of the elements and the Government. (Machinists continued to refer to the power source as 'the steam' long after conversion to electricity.) The management had to ask staff to put in extra time when the power was back on, to try to catch up with the orders that were waiting to be fulfilled. The machinists on piece work who had been losing out on their wages would have done their best to oblige.

The mood had been lightened in August 1947 when Noel Johnson married Elizabeth Hardy, only daughter of an electrical engineer from Lowestoft. Elizabeth was a self-motivated woman who had served in the Wrens during the war and learnt to drive on a milk float. Later she would help in the Johnson's firm, delivering materials to out-workers: the strain on her car, a Sunbeam Rapier, eventually caused the suspension to collapse.

The pair had met at a party of mutual friends – Noel was not, by his family's own admission, an especially handsome man but he was tall and kind and well-mannered; certainly a good match for the pretty, intelligent and well-to-do Miss Hardy.

The couple lived in Hopton

and then had their own new home built in the grounds of Flixton House where they would raise their two children in idyllic surroundings. Noel was very much a family man, and although he worked hard at the business he always had time for his wife, son Paul and daughter Susan who recalls, 'We used to have birthday parties to which other children were invited – in the garden if it was fine. On these occasions, he would come home from work for the afternoon and lay on various games.' At other times he would play 'cowboys and Indians' with the children, or take them fishing on the lake. Sometimes members of the extended family would visit and, says Susan, 'Where one or two Johnsons are gathered, there was always a cricket match! We all loved cricket.'

Noel had entered the company in 1945 and first had to learn as much as he could about the various manufacturing processes and the administration of the business from start to finish. He was taken under the wing of George Frederick Knights who was the younger brother of William George Knights, co-founder of Yarmouth Stores. George had started as an apprentice at Johnson & Sons in about 1890 and had stayed with them when the two companies had split and the two families had their differences of opinion. He worked his way up to the position of director and taught the young Noel Johnson everything he could. There was great sadness when George Knights died in 1950 at the age of 73; at the time he was still working as head of the cotton clothing department, which Noel then took over.

The final new recruit to the Johnson family firm was David Johnson, youngest son of Oswald and his second wife Marjorie 'Peggy', nee Cranswick.

Oswald and Peggy Johnson

Oswald had first married Ethel Gertrude Cole in 1906 but she had died seven years later, leaving Oswald with a young son named Arthur. At the end of the First World War Oswald met and married Marjorie, and the couple had another three children. Only David, the youngest, entered the business, but that was not until after his father had died at the age of 62. While David was away in the Royal Navy his parents had to leave their house on the seafront at Yarmouth and move inland to Bradfield near Reading. From there Oswald had travelled to the temporary factory at Leicester and also to Yarmouth where he would stay at the Queen's Hotel. One night as he was about to enter the hotel a bomb dropped nearby and soon after he suffered a heart attack. His health never fully recovered and he died at his home in November 1944.

Two years later, on Christmas Day, Frank Johnson also died suddenly. He had just started to cut back on his public duties and his son Russell had taken up his role as director at Johnson's earlier in the year. However his workload was still heavy and the stresses of wartime had taken their toll on his health. The funeral at St Peter's Church in Great Yarmouth was attended by the Mayor, numerous civic officials, and a host of friends and business associates, including representatives from Johnson & Sons Ltd.

Edwin was the only elder member of the family left to take the business forward, but his sons and nephews were there to lend support.

David returned from Naval service and joined the firm in 1946. He recalls, 'There was no pressure on me but I would have felt guilty if I didn't go in – Edwin and Frank had two sons in the business and my father had had none. I asked my Uncle Edwin if he could find me a job and he said I should learn the trade. I started at the hosiery factory at Admiralty Road and went on to spend two years learning the manufacturing methods in the knitwear, overall and shirt factories.'

In the article published in a magazine in November 1953 the reporter was shown the hosiery factory and wrote, '...by means of automatic and hand flat knitting machines, men's half hose, sea boot stockings, guernseys, sweaters and gloves are produced in considerable quantities. Although situated far from the centre of the hosiery industry, Johnson's have been able to train local labour to a high standard of efficiency in this highly skilled work and were able to keep their workers fully occupied during last year's period of poor trade arising from the drop in wool prices.'

As ever, the Johnsons' business activities were subject not only to the market but to the changing ideas and legislation of the government of the day, and at this time alterations in taxation had added to the confusion. By cutting prices on lower value fabrics it was possible to bring them into a tax free bracket within a new 'D scheme' and so customers were expecting reductions, even though manufacturers were still using up their stocks of higher-priced materials. Profits had fallen fast. Meanwhile committees and other organisations came and went; not least the short-lived Clothing Industry Development Council which many felt was ineffective and unjustifiably costly during its three year existence.[15]

Utility Clothing standards for civilians had been introduced in the war and continued until 1952 but in their 1953 catalogue Johnson & Sons Ltd suggested that the old Utility numbers which were intended as a guarantee of quality were still being used 'too freely nowadays on many qualities' and therefore they were introducing their own numbers alongside the Utility codes. That catalogue, printed in a basic, no-frills style with limited colour, carried the following introduction: '1941 was a long time ago – but the destruction of our Overall Factory then was a most difficult obstacle to get over. Everything was lost and it has taken years to rebuild – Years of shortage when we were unable to give you the Service we should have liked. But now in this Catalogue we feel we have a good range of Quality Products – Something for Everyone, and we hope you will find something which interests you.' The catalogue boasted the return of two pre-war favourites – bib and brace and boiler suits – brought back in blue heavy cotton twill and at a lower price.

---

[15] Information available at websites: http://www.theyworkforyou.com and http://hansard.millbanksystems.com

TWO PRE-WAR FAVOURITES

BLUE
BIB & BRACE

Pleated breast pocket with flap to button,
hammer sling, double rule pocket, two side
slant pockets, and bar tacked in red.
non-slip buckles, and bar tacked in red.

18/10

BLUE
R.A.F. BOILER
SUIT

A real quality Boiler Suit for the man
who wants the best.

30/-

RETURN TO SERVE YOU

The RIGHT GARMENTS at the RIGHT PRICE
made from a good quality
SANFORISED SHRUNK BLUE TWILL

BLUE
BIB & BRACE

Two shaped front patch pockets.
One hip and rule pocket.
One Pocket on bib.

14/-

R.A.F.
BOILER SUIT

Button through above waist.
Two pleated breast pockets.
Two side pockets.
One rule pocket.
All round belt.

23/8

2

3

Johnson's was making its own way in developing new products, and for the first time work wear specifically designed for women was being advertised, although there had been contracts during the war to supply overalls for the women's land army.

For
Work

LADIES' JEANS

Simply, but very Smartly cut with
Two Front-shaped Patch Pockets,
Belt Loops, and concealed Side Zip

THESE WILL SELL IN

6 ATTRACTIVE VAT SHADES 6
Fast to Light and Washing

LIGHT GREEN   BOTTLE GREEN   SAXE BLUE
ROYAL BLUE   RUST   MAROON   22—32 WAIST

14/11

or
Play

15

The company was also seeking out new and improved waterproofing methods. In the 1953 article the journalist reported, 'Following current demand, Johnson's are doing a considerable business in garments made from PVC proofed materials. In particular, these garments are finding greatest favour amongst yachtsmen and fishermen.'

Former employees say that the PVC material was lighter and easier to work with than the heavy oilskin, although some women suffered allergic reactions to the chemicals and, says one, 'the girls used to get boils on their arms when they made garments with it.'

The eminent scientist Dr Victor Yardsley, who pioneered the use of plastics in a vast range of applications, visited the factory a number of times and advised Russell Johnson on the development of the new materials. At around this time Russell was interviewed by Richard Dimbleby for the radio programme *Down Your Way*, and is pictured in this publicity shot sitting in his office, in February 1951.

The proofing process was a more delicate one than that used for oilskins. The PVC coating on the calico fabric had to be set at the correct temperature by means of infra red lamps. After the material had been stitched it had to be sealed using special welding machines. The reporter stated that the Admiralty had laid down rigid specifications for their contracts: 'that the fabric must withstand a flexing test of four hours at 300 flexions a minute through an angle of 180 degrees, without evidence of cracking or peeling of the coating from the base fabric.'

The factory had a laboratory equipped with a flexibility testing machine to ensure the requirement was met. Samples of clothing were sent out for testing and the article add ed that a fisherman's PVC frock had just been returned after 300 hours wear, and another had come back after 1,000 hours wear to be tested and evaluated.

Joy Hawkins's sister Pat had carried out her own impromptu test on a pair of the company's Holdfast overalls. Joy explained, 'She and her friend who was also called Pat, they were only 15 and just working as runabouts, they wanted to test out the saying "Bears any Strain". One got hold of one leg and the other got hold of one and they pulled – it came apart!' According to one former employee, there came a time when trading standards became stricter and Johnson's had to stop making the exaggerated claim about the strength of their clothing.

In 1944 the school leaving age had been raised to 15 and to comply with the Factories Acts of 1937 and 1948 Johnson's had to keep records of the fitness of people they employed who were under 18 years of age. They brought in basic regular medical examinations, the notes of which were kept in a standard-issue register. One woman who had to undergo a medical at the age of 16 recalls that she had to strip to the waist in a screened-off section of the canteen, with her assistant supervisor present. The girl was underweight for her age and she was mortified when she overheard her chaperone later commenting to another woman about the girls and their breast sizes.

As well as the fitness register the employers now had to record all 'Accidents and Dangerous Occurrences.' The book for the factory at Pier Plain, Gorleston still exists and bears testament to the hazards of working in the clothing manufacturing industry at that time. The men operating the band knives were not surprisingly at risk – there was no guard on the machine and they had to guide several layers of marked-up fabric through by hand. During the 1950s there were several incidences of cut fingers, but former employee Frank Greenwood remembers the day when his colleague George Angel severed his entire finger. Frank picked it up, but surgeons at the hospital were unable to sew it back on and George returned to work when his hand had healed over.

Joy Hawkins's sister Pat managed to sew a button on to her finger, and she also recalls that a new machine brought double trouble: 'On overalls we used to run and fell seams – where you've got a double seam up the leg, like on jeans, you had to lay them flat and fold them over so you'd do two rows of stitching. Then they got post machines that did all that in one go. But if you got your finger caught under that you got two needles in it.' The accident report book confirms this, with one entry showing that an employee suffered 'needles in finger' while working on the post machine.

Health and Safety began to become more of an issue at the factories of Johnson & Sons Ltd. There were other concerns, too – employers such as the Erie Resistor Company and Birds Eye were offering better rates of pay than Johnson's and many staff members were being tempted away. However, some employees remained loyal all their working lives: in August 1951 cutter Harry Halfnight completed 60 years' service and showed no sign of retiring.

Harry Charles Halfnight had been born to fisherman Samuel Halfnight and his wife Emma on 1st July 1878, and he grew up in the notoriously cramped and unhealthy atmosphere of the Rows. In the 1891 census the family were recorded as having moved to 66 Middlegate Street and at the age of 12 Harry was listed as being employed as a chemist's errand boy. His father was often away at sea but still his mother gave birth to a new baby almost every year – in the 1911 census, the first to record the number of children a couple had, Samuel declared that he had had fourteen children but eight of them had died. In fact by then his wife had also died, in 1905.

Harry had started working at Johnson's on 15th August 1891 and he told a newspaper reporter that he remembered John William Budds Johnson, the mayor of Yarmouth, being involved in the firm. In all, he would go on to work for three generations of the Johnson family.

His first job was applying oil to sou'westers at the oilskin factory. He recalled that when Edward VII's daughter Princess Maud of Wales married Prince Carl of Denmark (later King Haakon VII of Norway) in 1896, Johnson's presented her with two oil-silk coats and sou'westers; Harry had been the one to do the varnishing work on these coats. Next he was drafted in to help in the packing department because, he said, the firm was exporting oilskins to Australia and New Zealand, and the garments required special handling.

In the spring of 1900 Harry married Mary Ann Tiptod and their first son, also called Harry Charles, was born soon after. They had another son, Albert Edward, two years later. In that same year, 1902, Harry heard that the Johnson's overalls department was expanding and they needed new cutters to work on the dangerous band knives – he successfully applied and was still doing this job almost 50 years later. He had spent several years at Stockport when the firm had re-located there during the war.

Harry's achievement and loyal service were rewarded with a silver tankard and an ex-gratia payment, presented to him by the chairman Edwin Johnson. At the time Harry was 73 years old; by then he appears to have outlived all but one of his thirteen siblings, but he did see the arrival of his own grandchildren and great grandchildren. He was never a wealthy man: he and Mary Ann were living in a terraced house in Century Road, Southtown, and it must have seemed a world away from the terrible conditions in which Harry first saw life. He passed away in April 1956.

Harry Halfnight had also outlived his former boss Edwin Johnson, the elder statesmen of the firm, who died suddenly while getting dressed one morning in February 1953. He was aged 72.

Edwin's death brought an end to the generation that had brought Johnson & Sons Ltd through the first half of the twentieth century and through two world wars. There had been significant changes during the past two decades and it is known that the firm had struggled financially at times. Edwin had had to mortgage his own home, Flixton House, and had sold other property to raise money which he put into the business. He was able to repay the mortgage when trade improved. In the meantime his brother Oswald had introduced a personal friend to the brothers, and it had been agreed that John Elliott Coney could buy shares and become a director of Johnson & Sons Ltd, although he does not seem to have played a major role in the running of the firm.

Coney had been born in 1886, had fought in the First World War with the Royal Norfolk regiment and had subsequently seen service in Kenya. He had been engaged in coffee growing and had returned to England in 1926, living for a time in Southwold, Suffolk. He joined Johnson's the following year. Later he moved to Beccles and was elected Mayor for four terms from 1947. He was still a director of Johnson's at that time, and continued as a director for at least another twenty years, including twelve as Chairman.[16]

---

[16] Johnson & Sons Ltd Statement of Accounts 1965 and *Beccles & Bungay Times* archive at
www.foxearth.org.uk/BecclesAreaNewspapers/Newspapers1947complete.html

John Coney was possibly the first person who was not a family member to invest in Johnson's and to hold shares and a directorship. It is likely that there had been some reluctance to admit him, but in hard times it had become a necessity to bring in fresh capital. This relinquishment of some degree of control was an admission that the Johnson family were finding it increasingly difficult to maintain their past successes and rate of growth, but they were not prepared to give up without a fight.

Chapter Six

Weathering the changes

By the end of the 1950s society was changing rapidly and yet the managers of Johnson & Sons Ltd seemed determined to hold firm in their traditional ways of handling the company. 'We were very conservative,' says David Johnson.

Much of their business still involved a reliance on trust, which was not always well placed. For a time they rented an office in London simply as a postal address, and paid an agent to visit regularly to collect the letters. Noel happened to be in London one day and called round to check the property; he found that he could hardly push the door open because a mountain of post had accumulated behind it, and it became clear that their agent had been nowhere near the premises. They gave up the lease.

Business deals sometimes required extra incentives and the Johnsons had to accept that to gain contracts one had to play the game. A former employee recalls that when inspectors or businessmen came to the factories they would often expect to leave with a quantity of clothing wrapped up in a brown paper parcel under their arm.

Great Yarmouth itself was becoming a magnet for holidaymakers, and as the holiday camps sprouted along the coast the fishing industry continued to decline. Customers for the Johnsons' products were becoming mostly land-based; Doris Porter, who started work at the Conge factory in 1955 recalls the lines that she worked on. 'We made jeans, although only for workmen at first. There were coats for the G.P.O., boiler suits for B.E.A., clothing for Birdseye, J.A. Rank, Colmans, and Denny's of London. Also jackets for British Rail, shorts and trousers for the Navy, and fishermen's jumpers in drill cotton.'

Doris had started work at the age of 15 and like her colleagues she had been a 'runabout' first, sorting bundles of fabric pieces and generally running errands for the girls on the machines. Her first wage was £2 4 /6 ½d a week. Soon she was given the chance to do machining; she worked on the conveyor belt which ran the length of the factory, taking garments through the stages of manufacture to the final stage at the end when the buttons and buttonholes were completed.

The forewoman was Ethel Chubbock, who had previously worked in the silk factory, presumably Grout's. She was aged 60 by then, but there was no requirement to retire at a set age. Her contemporaries and fellow forewomen were Evelyn Crowe, a 'tiny but formidable' lady, and Doris South. None of these ladies married but each lived to a ripe age: 83, 94 and 86 years respectively.

There were mixed feelings about the conveyor belt system. As the women were paid according to how many garments they made, frustration could soon build up if one or two of their colleagues were slower and held up the production line. There were a few 'spats' on occasion, says Doris, but in general the atmosphere was friendly and the girls would sing along to the radio, especially with programmes such as Music While You Work on the BBC. 'Girls used to swoon whenever Dickie Valentine came on, or when it was Bobby Vinton singing *Blue Velvet*,' she recalls.

At Christmas the factory would be decorated with paper chains, many of them wrapped perilously round light fittings and electric machines. On the last working day before the holidays the girls could finish work at midday and enjoy a few drinks.

The following photos of the factory at the Conge were taken in December 1952.

Above: the conveyor belt can be seen in the front left of the picture

Below: forewoman Miss Stella Bullock (standing on right of foreground) oversees work on the conveyor belt

The colleagues at Great Yarmouth organised dances at the Floral Hall Ballroom, but, says Doris, one year it had to be cancelled because the floor was found to be rotten. 'They had booked Victor Sylvester to play there - it was a shame we couldn't see him,' she says.

By 1958 Johnson & Sons were starting to take notice of fashions and in addition to work wear jeans they began to make 'pedal pushers' – cropped trousers for women. Three girls from the factory were chosen to model the outfits at the National Boat Show, Olympia, including Barbara Thurtle nee Robinson, (right) who was then only 15 at the time, and Myrtle Rix.

In a newspaper cutting from around this period, the journalist reported, 'Until recent years the factory specialised in ordinary protective clothing such as coats and overalls of various types in heavy cottons. But when the American "jean" craze spread to Britain, Johnson's were quick to realise the possibilities of the craze for "casual" wear. Altogether there are about 2800 permutations in type, size and colour in the men's range of garments and 650 different types of women's wear produced at this one factory.' The factory in question was the one on the corner of the Conge and North Quay, which was in the process of being extended.

The mood at Johnson's was upbeat and at Pier Plain, Gorleston, a family atmosphere reigned. Pauline Edwards nee Wilson started work there in September 1961. Her mother took her in to meet Miss Beattie Williams the forewoman at Gorleston and, says Pauline, 'I don't know what sort of person I was expecting, but it wasn't a stocky, middle-aged woman with greying hair and a slight stoop. She had a gruff voice but she smiled and said, "Hello ol' dear, what can I do for you?" After Mum explained that I wanted a job Miss Williams said, "Well then ol' dear you can start 8.15 tomorrow morning." And I did.'

Beattie Williams was in charge of the machine room with Gladys Farman her deputy: a small, elderly woman with tight-permed hair and glasses. The pair stood at a table overlooking the factory floor, watching all the women at their work. Pauline recalls, 'The room was very big with three long benches with twelve machines either side. The other part of the room there were individual sewing machines that did specialised work, such as making buttonholes or sewing on buttons.'

The busy, noisy factory floor was a frightening prospect for a shy young girl but Pauline soon found that the older women were kind and helpful to the point of being motherly towards her, and she began to settle in.

Above (left to right): Doris Brown nee Farman, Pauline Edwards nee Wilson, Phyllis Collins nee Atkins, Margaret Mills, 1963

As a 'runabout' Pauline had to return any substandard work to machinists and ask them to do the work again, which meant unpicking the offending seam and re-stitching it. Sometimes the women had gone on to a different type of garment and changed the colour of thread in their machine, so they would have to change it back to fix the offending seam. Naturally this was never welcome, as 'time was money.'

One of the women who befriended Pauline was June Willison nee Kippen, who sympathised with her feelings. 'When we started there we were all young and very naive and scared,' she says, and Pauline agrees. 'I was naive – if anyone told a joke I'd go red as a beetroot.' Good-natured comments from the men in the cutting room caused Pauline a great deal of embarrassment at first but, she adds, 'after a few weeks I got used to them.'

June insists there was never 'bad language' in the factory, although perhaps the odd swear word could be expected when a piece of work had gone wrong. The noise from the machines was such that the women had to raise their voices to talk to each other, or to mouth words, and some found it a hard habit to break when outside the work place.

The women at Gorleston had numerous social groups organised, and clubs whereby they could pay in weekly amounts and take turns to have money for a hairdo, or clothing or even premium bonds. They organised dinner-dances at some of the popular venues of the time, such as Gunton Hall and the Floral Hall in Gorleston, and their boss Noel was invited to join them.

Pauline says, 'About September Beattie Williams would start her weekly raffles. We all put in two shillings a week and she would buy six small prizes for the Monday draw. But she would keep some money back and then we all got something in the big Christmas raffle.'

Above: Noel Johnson (with pipe) and his wife Elizabeth attending a Christmas function, December 1961

June had started at Johnson's in 1944 and she and her colleagues had enjoyed some harmless high jinks. In the photo on the right June, far right, is wearing a pair of men's trousers she has just made.

June recalls that the machinists wore flowery wrap-around aprons bought at the Co-op and, she says, 'they used to get worn out on the bust line and we had to patch them.' In the picture below, June's colleague Margaret Olley, now sadly deceased, can be seen (far left) wearing a turban – 'Sometimes we wore those because we were going out later and had curlers in our hair,' June explains.

The girls could be even more daring when it came to adding the finishing touch to bib and brace overalls. 'We had to put big cardboard labels on them, the Holdfast label, it had to be stitched on the back pocket. We used to write our name and address on the reverse – I don't think anyone ever got a reply.' In 1946 June would meet her future husband at a 'Victory in Japan' (V.J.) Day party in Great Yarmouth. They married five years later.

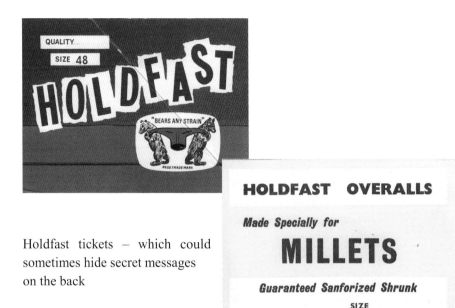

Holdfast tickets – which could sometimes hide secret messages on the back

Like many others June was lured away to work for Erie Resistors who paid higher wages, but she was never happy there and after she married and had a child she returned to Johnson's. When her son was a teenager in the 1960s, flared or 'bell bottomed' jeans became the height of fashion and June says that she was allowed to take home off-cuts of blue denim to make his flares wider still. The heavyweight denim and khaki drill materials were hard to sew and girls were supplied with a small piece of soap or candle wax to rub on the machine needle and ease it through. They had to be careful not to damage the fabric.

When June finally left Johnson's for good it was with a great deal of sadness, but she stayed in contact with old friends and continued to use her sewing skills at home, making clothes and curtains and cushion covers. 'I never forgot my Johnson's days and never will,' she says.

June with friends from Johnson's

Pauline continued working at the Pier Plain factory into the 1970s, and would be witness to less happy times as the family firm of Johnson & Sons Ltd was entering its final phase.

In November 1962 a large portion of the oilskin factory at Admiralty Road was badly damaged by fire. The blaze broke out in the early hours of Sunday the 18th, and it was fortunate that police officers passing by in a patrol car had seen smoke coming from the building and raised the alarm. Four fire appliances rushed to the scene, nine hoses were brought to bear on the building and two firemen were injured as they tackled the fire and dense, choking smoke. One fell through a fanlight and was hauled out by colleagues and taken to hospital; the other was overcome by smoke but he recovered quickly and went back to help tackle the fire.

A newspaper report explained that the fire was in the north end of the building, and all three floors were affected: the top floor was not in use, but on the first floor there were garments awaiting welding of the seams and a quantity of oilskin linings were hung out in lines. There was also a laboratory, which was partly damaged. On the ground floor there were oilskins and drums of linseed oil as well as cardboard cartons for packing. Where the process of treating the fabric with oil had gone on for decades, the floorboards were impregnated with linseed oil.

Above: photo from *Eastern daily Press*

The oilskin itself was highly flammable, as more than one employee has commented – Peggy Driver used to take off-cuts to burn on the fire at home. One newspaper report stated that there had previously been a major fire at the oilskin factory in 1913, when £10,000 worth of damage had been caused.[17]

Former chief mechanic Ronnie Webb recalls that the stacks of oilskin fabric could heat up of their own accord, but as the news report stated, there had also been a fire in a nearby factory less than a week ago. It was possible that arsonists were at work. In any case, the quick action of the emergency services had meant that the main factory area

---

[17] *Great Yarmouth Mercury* 5 September 2003

had been saved and a spokesman for the Johnsons, presumably Russell, insisted 'Production will not be affected at all.'[18]

'Mr Russell' as the staff called him, was manager of the oilskin factory at Admiralty Road and it seems he had hoped that his only son would follow in his footsteps, but in that year Malcolm Johnson was ordained as a minister and would pursue his vocation in the Church of England.

Russell's brother Gordon remained in charge of the hosiery factory on the opposite side of Admiralty Road. He had married and had one daughter, who was not expected to take up a role in the company. As mentioned, Michael died in 1961 without having had any children, and Noel, managing director based at The Conge, had a son and daughter who did not join the firm. David, the youngest cousin, did not have a place on the board of directors but was managing the shirt factory. He had married Gill Dyas in 1963 and moved to rural Suffolk to raise a family, commuting to Gorleston each day.

All of the Johnsons must have been aware of this shortage of successors, and they were about to face a raft of new challenges. In 1965 Corporation Tax had been introduced and in the Directors' Report and Statement of Accounts for the end of the year the chairman Russell Johnson warned, 'The effect of the 1965 tax legislation will be felt fully in the current year and, assuming the present rate of dividend is maintained, in future the balance available to place to reserves will be considerably less.'

The dividend had been set at 5% and the report notes, 'The Trading profit of the Company has increased by £7,000 and although the rate of Corporation Tax has not yet been announced it is considered wise to provide for this at the rate of 40%.'

In the figures, large cumulative sums had been written off the value of the machinery, plant, fixtures, motors and office furniture, originally costing £160,701 now leaving a net value of £32, 285. The freehold and

---

[18] *Eastern Daily Press* 19 November 1962

leasehold properties including premises at Norwich had been devalued from their original cost of £131,048 to £70,000. The amount owed by debtors and including advance payments came to £135,885 and Johnson's owed its creditors £103,695.

Russell added, 'Full production is being maintained and the volume of orders on hand is encouraging but the Company is again faced by further increases in costs as a result of recent trade agreement for higher wages, increased holidays, and a shorter working week, which with other increased manufacturing expenses makes it very difficult to keep overhead expenses at a reasonable figure. The shareholders are assured that the Board continues to make every effort to increase productivity and effect economies and will do its utmost to maintain the present rate of dividend.' Russell ended with a note of thanks to all of the employees.

It was clear that the good times were over. On 15th February 1971 the United Kingdom completed its conversion to decimalisation, and the Johnsons had had to prepare themselves in advance. The Autumn price list for 1970 contained prices in shillings and pence and also in decimal currency, but the sizes were still in inches. Soon they would have to show those in centimetres as well. At the same time discussions were taking place that would finally enable the U. K. to join the European Economic Community, and Value Added Tax was on the horizon.

Apart from these modern advances in commerce there were other, more pressing concerns. The cost of producing their own 'NZ' waxed fabric had become so high that the Johnsons had found it more economical to import the cloth, although it is unlikely that the quality would have been of the same standard. But market forces were too strong to resist, and Johnson's had to follow where their customers led. David Johnson recalls, 'The work shirts we were producing were quite expensive compared to others that were available. We began to buy in some cheaper-end shirts that were made in China. I'm afraid it was what some of our customers wanted.'

Traditional customers such as the miners and fishermen were fighting a losing battle to keep their industries going. The armed forces were being steadily reduced and government contracts were harder to come by. The Johnsons were having to look to the leisure industry for new customers, and it was unfamiliar territory.

The firm did not have the resources to invest in new machinery and it was losing staff to those firms that paid higher wages. There was still a core band of women who were devoted to Johnson's – as Pauline Edwards says, 'The money wasn't good but there was job satisfaction and we were happy, and that meant more than just the money.'

Goodwill and staff satisfaction could not keep the Johnson firm afloat: when outsiders started to make moves to buy up shares in the company, a takeover began to seem inevitable.

Chapter Seven

The Lesser takeover

On 6th September 1972 a letter was sent by Parker, Thomas & Co, a London solicitor, to all the shareholders of Johnson & Sons Ltd, advising them of an offer to buy their shares. The client was J.E. Lesser & Sons (Holdings) Ltd of Hounslow, and they were making the very attractive offer of £1.67 ½ per £1 share. There was a condition attached, that the hosiery factory at Admiralty Road would be sold off the following year, although it promised that a share of the proceeds would be distributed.

It added, 'It is the acquiring Company's intention to continue the business as heretofore and they will retain the Company's employees. Funds required for the running of the business are available.'

In a breakdown of the Directors' shares it showed that Noel held the highest number at almost 36,000 with Gordon holding over 31,000, Russell had over 25,000 and the firm's secretary Kenneth Westney held 5,000.

Accompanying the offer was a separate letter from Russell, the Chairman, advising the shareholders to accept. He stated, 'Your Board has considered offers for the Company during the past few years but has not had a previous offer worthy of the shareholders' consideration. The present offer is conditional upon the present management continuing in the business and is, in the Board's opinion, the best means of ensuring continuity of the company.' Russell confirmed that the directors would be selling their own shares; a sufficient majority of the outside investors followed, amounting to over 90 per cent take up.

The news was soon out. 'Clothing factories sold: jobs pledge' summarised the *Great Yarmouth Mercury* headline on 13th October.

The report said the directors had given an assurance that the sale would be a 'buttress, not a threat, to the jobs of the 540 Norfolk employees.' Similar statements were made on behalf of Lesser's, which was quoted as paying £½ million for the firm. The branch of Lesser's which would include Johnson's was called Jeltek Ltd, and while the parent company was mainly concerned with property and development, Jeltek, one of nine subsidiaries, was promoted as a 'leading manufacturer of industrial and leisure outdoor wear,' with a factory at Halbeath, Fife. The deal was finalised and changes swiftly followed.

Gordon Johnson, who had run the hosiery factory, retired, although he had already spent several years battling cancer. He was a quiet, reserved man and is remembered by his daughter Ann as being modest, generous and with a strong social conscience. She adds, 'He hated to see any injustice and helped many people during his relatively short life.' Her father had joined the army when she was a baby and when he came home on leave in 1940 the little girl screamed as this strange man in khaki uniform tried to greet her.

Right: Gordon with Ann, 1940

Having returned to duty Gordon suffered a burst appendix while on parade one day and was in hospital for weeks, culminating in a discharge from the Army. His relationship with his daughter became closer over the years but of course, being a girl, Ann was never expected to take an active part in the Johnsons' firm.

Gordon lost his battle against cancer on 7th January 1978.

Russell became vice chairman in 1972 as Lesser's brought in Maurice Soffa to replace him as chairman, along with two other new directors. Noel Johnson became a senior executive director and also had a place on the board of Jeltek. David Johnson, who until then had simply been an employee of the family firm, was now a director.

Cyril Lesser stated that new ideas would be needed in the future to meet rapid changes in customers' tastes, but changes would be 'gradual, carefully thought out and discussed and agreed with Johnson's directors.' It all seemed to be the best that could be expected under the circumstances and Noel emphasised again that it was their firm belief that the deal would make employees' futures more secure.

It had already been agreed that the hosiery factory would be sold, and this was completed the following year. The machinery had earlier been moved across to the oilskin works, but now it was decided that hosiery production should cease and manager John Winterburn bought up the equipment. He started a new company, the Great Yarmouth Knitting Co Ltd, and employed a number of former Johnson's workers.

True to their word, the new management at Johnson's was busy looking at ways to increase sales and in 1973 they announced a drive to export their products to E.E.C. countries under a new company name, Jeltex Johnson Exports Ltd. A news cutting stated that the combined turnover of the companies Jeltek and Johnson's was more than £2.8 million and they expected exports to increase by 50% in the coming year. Deals would be handled through an agent in Holland, who would answer to the Lesser bosses in Hounslow. Complementary products from manufacturers other than Jeltek and Johnson's would also be sold through this route.

The newcomers were seen as 'whizz kids' by the older incumbents at Johnson's and this was by no means such a bad thing all round. With smarter marketing experience the managers embraced the upcoming cult of celebrity and secured world famous footballer Geoff Hurst to promote their sports wear. Lesser's in-house newsletter dated Spring 1974 carried a lengthy one-sentence paragraph that explained, 'Among the hosts at a reception to introduce the new Johnson Flag range of sports and leisure wear was Stoke and England footballer, Geoff Hurst, who is a graduate of the Tailor and Cutter Academy, and is now Director of Design for Johnsons Sports and Leisure Wear Division which markets a range of garments, including track suits, tennis wear, knitwear, shirts and outdoor activity clothing under the crossed flags symbol.'

It is unknown how much time Hurst actually spent working on designs for Johnson's, although he and fellow footballer Alan Hudson did pay a visit to the clothing factories and many of the staff members were keen to have their photo taken with the famous sportsmen.

Right: Geoff Hurst signing autographs for Phyllis Noble and Pauline Edwards, 1973

On this page: with staff at the Conge, Great Yarmouth

Above: Geoff Hurst and Alan Hudson with Joy Hawkins (left) and Joan Tubby
Below: with cutter Bob Nicholls

In the same newsletter Lesser's announced that they were in the process of building their sixth store for F.W. Woolworth and Co Ltd, and had secured a large contract for building council houses in Shropshire. They had also bought up a German construction firm, and had invested £1 million in a land deal in America.

It is clear that the firm's core experience was in property matters rather than clothing manufacture. Even so, during this time round-the-world yachtsman Robin Knox-Johnston was hired too, and new catalogues stated that he had helped the firm develop their new range of sailing wear, including an ocean racing range. There were track suits and anoraks, and another new line was introduced: weatherproof clothing for motorcyclists, although this would not prove to be a long term success.

Above: cover of 1970s sailing wear catalogue with Jeltek logo

Above and below: the 1975 catalogue, photographed around Great Yarmouth, shows the new direction the firm was taking in aiming for the leisure wear market

Golden, shimmering sand as far as the eye can see. Pretty girls in bikinis . . . tiny-tots with buckets and spades . . . melting ice-cream . . . Dad in rolled-up trousers. The informal gaiety of Great Yarmouth spills down to the very water's edge. It is little wonder that Johnsons *do so* like to be beside the seaside.

At the Norwich factory staff had to re-train in order to work on the new range of motorcycle and sailing clothing. At the same time the company ceased proofing its own PVC fabrics and used an outside firm to provide its waterproof material including waxed cotton.

Unfortunately Johnson's suffered from mistakes that cost them vital orders: they had tried using a lighter weight PVC cloth, but the quality had declined and complaints had soared. The staff were unhappy too: 'the material got thinner and thinner,' said one former machinist. In a 1975 management report it was stated 'PVC stocks are suffering from the bad reputation in the trade of our garments made from 6oz cloth. We are finding it increasingly difficult to sell 6oz although the demand continues to be high for 8oz.' The company took steps to appease its customers but was still left with a large stock of the cheaper fabric that nobody wanted.

The new team now began to introduce a very different management style compared to the democratic, familial relationship that had previously existed between the employers and employees at Johnson's. They handed supervisors a booklet produced by the Trades Union Congress entitled *An Outline of Work Study and Payment by Results* which revealed their plan: in the introduction it stated, '...considerable and growing attention is already paid to securing the most effective use of resources – whether capital, plant, materials or manpower. Work study is prominent among the means used for these purposes...'[19]

The first steps outlined in the booklet were to define the job to be studied and then time a typical worker at the task. This meant installing clocks on the girls' machines, although at least one flatly refused, and was called up to the office where she made her feelings very clear. She was not one of the ones who were timed.

Doris Porter, who was working at the Conge factory says, 'Nobody liked the time and motion study. But the some of the girls worked hard to show off what they could do – and of course that made it bad for

---

[19] Booklet first published by the T.U.C. June 1963 this revised ed. February 1968

them, that set the standard.' As expectations were raised, women began to leave although Doris stayed with a resigned feeling of 'better the devil you know.'

Many staff had been at Johnson's for too long to contemplate moving: in 1973 Eddie Burman, who for much of his career had been Noel's 'right hand man,' had received a clock in recognition of 40 years' service. Others who had stayed for four decades were: John Bracey, Ralph Bowles, Orris Daines, Ruby Frost, Eric Hunn, Leonard Manthorpe, Ethel Nichols, Lily Utting, Jack Utting, Stanley Weldon, and Aggie Wilding.

Peggy Driver and Ronnie Webb were among those to receive awards for 25 years' service, along with Mollie Annis, Sheila Barham, Laura Blyth, Betty Codling, Alice Cooke, Gordon Godbolt, Phyllis Hewitt, Gladys Newark, George Nichols, John Palmer, Daphne Parrot, Adelaide Philpott, Brian Riches, Joy Riches, Joan Simnett, Ethel Spyers, Evelyn Storey, Norman Taylor, Dolly Thurston, Edna Woodcock, Gordon Wood, Fred Wrath and Marjorie Wright.

This loyalty had been mutual, but those days were coming to an end. The Johnson family members were no more comfortable with the changes than their staff, but at first they refused to go voluntarily. David Johnson admits he was not enthusiastic in his support of the new managers, but he says the new practices were unfamiliar to his family: 'They wanted all these reports about everything – we had never done reports before, we'd kept records of figures of course, but mostly we discussed things and got on with them. One day I attended a meeting, it went on for three hours but at the end of it I couldn't see what had been decided.' David was told that in fact he was not entitled to attend further meetings, and had to prove that as a director it was his right to do so.

In the meantime Russell Johnson's son Malcolm discovered that in the boardroom the portraits of the firm's founder John William Johnson and his wife Caroline, as well as the highly respected former chairman, Arthur Herbert Johnson, had been taken down and replaced with a picture of Mr Lesser. The family portraits had been put out for disposal but were rescued by the family and taken home.

In his early career David had been on the road for several years, building up a sales area in the home counties but he had progressed to the job of manager in charge of the travellers and the larger accounts. He had been manager of the shirt factory for twelve years but after the take over he had been given the title 'temporary marketing director', a sphere in which he had no particular experience. However when he was given the task of providing information for an article that was to appear in Men's Wear magazine in July 1975, he was glad to oblige. The feature duly appeared with the title 'The past is still present in East Anglia.'[20]

Starting with the incorrect statement that Johnson's was now part of the 'Lessing' Group, it went on to say that the company constituted 'a strong flavour of English turn-of-the century life' although with 'plenty of up-to-the-minute ideas and products.' The entire first page was devoted to a potted history of the company, with quotations and pictures from the 1905 catalogue that is still in David's possession.

Finally the journalist turned to the present, adding, 'There is a division dealing with world championship tennis gear, part of the name-merchandising which figures so strongly in modern sport. Geoff Hurst promotes their football gear. Mick Andrews, the Ace trials rider, promotes their brilliantly designed motor-bike suit in polyurethane nylon.'

He emphasised that old favourites such as collarless shirts were going through a revival, and demands for traditional farm workers' clothing prevented the firm from withdrawing them from production. Furthermore it had once again become economical to make NZ waxed cloth in-house and so 'Machines in a Victorian factory, long unused are being brought back into service'.

The closing paragraphs ran, 'Old skills, old ways, old values, shouldn't be thrown out too casually: often enough, the need for them

---

[20] *Men's Wear* published by Textile Trade Publications Ltd issue 3807

returns more quickly than was imagined. Wally Turner, who started long ago on this ancient machinery, and has since mastered the plastics-age equipment of PVC making, is returning to the huge drying rooms and turn-of-the-century machinery of a technology which most probably thought would never be needed again. When I saw him re-acquainting himself with the old buildings he was like a child with a *new* toy: not one which had lain obsolete for years. Old pleasures die hard.'

This double-page spread, which the new 'whizz kid' management thought would promote the go-ahead attitude of the firm, had instead portrayed them as charming, old-fashioned and adhering to the past. David had been proud to share the heritage of Johnson & Sons: Lessers were inclined to sweep all that away and say 'that was then, this is now.'

In spite of being a director, David was now seen as someone who did not subscribe to the ethos of the firm and it was suggested that he might like to take up a more peripatetic role. The firm's area representative for East Anglia had recently retired and David was asked to take on the job – it was effectively a demotion, but one he accepted. It was a relief to get out of the office and engage with their customers once more.

At the end of October a list of the firm's representatives showed the following areas of responsibility:

South West – Mr A. Lisk;
South East – Mr M. Forster;
East Anglia – Mr G. Holland (followed by David Johnson);
E. Midlands – Mr R. Welsby;
W. Midlands – Mr W. Ford;
N. England – Mr C. MacNeil;
Gtr London – Mr V. Raven;
N. England – Mr S. Jones.

There were also agents in Cornwall, Scotland, Northern Ireland and the Channel Island, and specialists agents selling the sports and leisure wear garments.

Each of the representatives was expected to bring in business that amounted to tens of thousands of pounds per year, and they succeeded to a greater or lesser degree. However a 1975 management report stated, 'Reports coming back from the Salesmen have, for a long time now, stated quite definitely that the traditional Johnson retailer is in decline. 3000 accounts in 1973 reduced to 2000 accounts in 1975. The Retailer who has traded upwards is surviving, the multiples like Milletts are doing the real business and will continue to do so.'

The report highlighted that price was crucial in attracting sales, and the pressure would continue to mount on staff both in the factories and out on the road to reduce costs and maximise profits.

Above: David Johnson, third right, attending the retirement dinner of sales representative Gilbert Holland in 1975. Gilbert (centre) cuts a cake; to his right is the then chairman of Johnson's, Maurice Soffa

Noel Johnson remained in an office at the Conge, but with his manners, principles and appearance reminiscent of another era, he did not fit comfortably in the new regime. He had a devoted secretary in Celia Ebbage nee Styles, who had been born in London near the Old Kent Road in 1916 during an air raid. Her father having been gassed during the war, the family had moved to the clearer air of Gorleston and Celia had worked as a legal secretary for 37 years before being asked to work for Noel. She too had a sharp mind and photographic memory; she had become passionate about the heritage, art and landscape of Norfolk and had married local accountant and artist George Ebbage, who sadly died after just 16 years of marriage. Celia kept busy organising exhibitions of George's work and promoting local causes, and later in her obituary it was said 'As a local historian, Celia loved old buildings but had a special gift for recalling the networks of families and friends which are the bricks and mortar of living communities.'[21]

Between them, Noel and Celia represented an oasis of old-fashioned common sense and compassion in the new, brash, bright and synthetic world. Neither could approve of all the changes happening to the business and its staff but both were powerless to object. Finally, in 1977, Noel was asked to leave.

Johnson's enormous loss would become the gain of the Yarmouth Stores for Noel wrote to the then chairman and it was agreed that former years of antipathy notwithstanding, the time was right for a reconciliation between the Johnsons and the Knights family. Noel became a part-time consultant and took with him a wealth of experience and contacts which meant that a number of customers and their business followed him.

The move gave Noel the freedom to pursue his other interests and as well as enjoying shooting, fishing, watching cricket and playing golf, he was now able to become ever more involved in local health matters. He worked tirelessly on a campaign to build a new hospital at Gorleston for

---

[21] *Great Yarmouth Mercury* 23 December 2011

the people of East Anglia and faced down a great deal of opposition before The Department of Health gave its approval in 1976. However there would be another six years of negotiation and hard work before the scheme came to fruition and the new James Paget Hospital finally opened its doors. In a newspaper tribute it said, 'Under his leadership as the chairman of the Great Yarmouth and Waveney Health Authority the Paget was designed, built and commissioned, and opened in two phases in the early 1980s.'[22]

There was one last hurdle to overcome: on the day of the official opening in July 1982 the country was experiencing a national strike and the Mayor of Great Yarmouth refused to cross the picket line. Nevertheless the guest of honour Professor Dorothy Crowfoot did attend and performed the opening ceremony.[23]

Noel continued to work for all of the local patients and the community at large and held other public offices including Deputy Lieutenant of Suffolk. He was awarded the MBE in 1987. Failing health eventually brought him to the James Paget Hospital as a patient, but he was still more concerned about the staff and other patients than himself. He died there on 13th December 2005 at the age of 82.

Noel Johnson 1923 - 2005

[22] *East Anglian Daily Times* 26 December 2005
[23] Information from James Paget Hospital website
http://www.jpaget.nhs.uk/section.php?id=76

Without their flexible and understanding boss Noel on their side, the staff at Johnson's found that things changed rapidly in the late 1970s. First, older employees were no longer allowed to continue working for as long as they liked but were asked to retire, and a raft of farewell announcements in the local newspaper followed.

In June 1977 Mrs Lily Cooke retired after 41 years' service and was presented with a clock by Gorleston managing director Brian Evans who said that he knew Lily loved dress-making – she could sew a complete shirt in 20 minutes – and that she had regarded her time at Johnson's as a hobby. Two weeks earlier Miss Gladys Harwen had also left, having completed 44 years' service. Ernest Laycock was given a gold watch when he left after working for Johnson's for 46 years and the irrepressible Brian Evans described him as 'a likeable guy with a flexible attitude'.

In October 1977 Mrs Molly Bullock, a quality control inspector at Pier Plain, retired after 21 years' service and received a carriage clock, presented by production manager John Thorpe who praised her 'cheerfulness and vitality.' Mrs Terry Bird had left three weeks earlier and received a rose bowl in recognition of 12 years at Johnson's.

In addition to the retirements, staff were leaving because they found that under the new targets set as a result of the work study exercises, they could no longer earn as much money. A production line system was brought in and a machinist could find herself stitching nothing but pockets for days on end, severely reducing their enjoyment in their work. Still a great number stayed, but worse was to come.

David Johnson had been finding that customers were less happy with the new regime; they felt that since Johnson's had changed hands the service they received had deteriorated. David fed back their comments and in a letter sent to him at the end of 1977 the chairman Cyril Lesser confirmed that, having visited the factories for the first time in 18 months, he would attend to the concerns.

In the first week of January 1978 it was announced that Lesser's had sold their shares in Johnson & Sons to Scottish-based leisure and industrial group Black & Edgington. It was reported that 450 men and women were currently employed in the premises at Yarmouth, Gorleston and Norwich. A spokeman said that being part of Black & Edgington, who had a thriving clothing and workwear division called Clares Carlton Ltd, would be 'beneficial to us rather than being part of a construction company.' The spokesman also told journalists that no changes were envisaged in the foreseeable future, and everything would 'stay as it is at the moment.'

Three weeks later it emerged that the factory at Pier Plain, Gorleston, was to close. The employees were told the news, and, says former supervisor Hazel Tucker, 'the girls went outside and sat on the steps, we were all so sad we didn't know what to say.'

The message from management remained upbeat and Brian Evans insisted that the move was necessary as part of a drive to 'cut down the operating costs without cutting the manpower.' The future of the firm was bright, he said, as Black & Edgington had its own retail shops and their market share in work clothing was three times the size of Johnson's sales. He described the factory closure as 'a relatively painless business,' with 17 employees being made redundant and the rest – just over 100 – being offered jobs at North Quay and Admiralty Road. Free transport was to be laid on from Gorleston, with machinists going to The Conge and the cutting room equipment and staff transferring to Admiralty Road.

Over 170 miles of fabric, 150 sewing machines and several 70 foot cutting tables had to be re-located with minimum disruption to production. The move took place at the end of February and it was an emotional time for the staff who worked there. One anonymous artist drew the cartoon that follows, depicting the move. It was the one ray of brightness in an otherwise gloomy process.

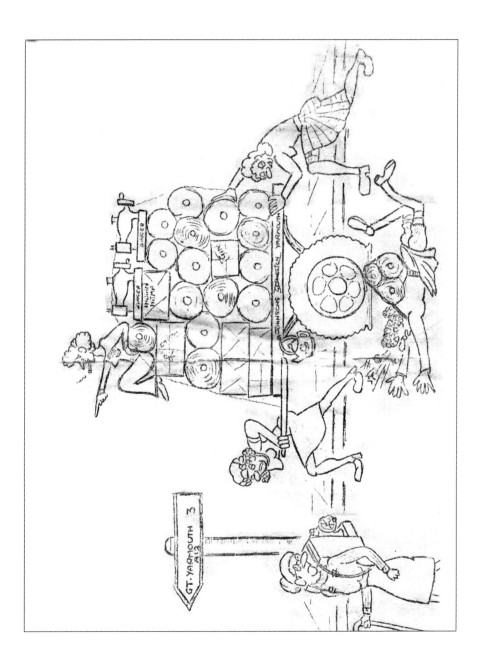

Chapter Eight

The Final Years

Joy Hawkins recalls, 'When we went from Gorleston to Yarmouth the atmosphere wasn't very hot. Some of the girls had come from Admiralty Road as well; they pushed us all together, they had oilskins and shirts and a blue room where they made overalls, and a proper training room for machinists.'

The latter was run by Doreen Jones and Hazel Tucker. Doreen, nee Aldred, had started at Johnson's shirt factory in Gorleston in 1945 but had taken a break after she married, travelling with her husband who was in the Marines, and she returned to work when her daughter was at secondary school. As a young girl she had once dawdled on the way to work, window shopping, and when she arrived just a few minutes late she had found that the forewoman Miss South had locked her out. She was allowed in but was docked 15 minutes from her pay – 'I never did it again' she says.

Hazel Tucker, who had started at Pier Plain in 1950 also took breaks in her career when her children were born and for a short-lived emigration to Australia, after which she came back to Johnson's and was made a supervisor. With Doreen Jones, Hazel was put in charge of the training section and she says, 'I taught girls on all types of machines – sewing, buttonholes, post machines – a lot of the girls were very good. The worst part was having to tell those who weren't up to scratch, they couldn't make the grade and so they had to go.'

Under the new management it was harder than ever to live up to expectations in terms of productivity, and it was no longer the case that any girl or woman could walk into Johnson's and be virtually guaranteed a job. The company was going through a major re-organisation, and that meant that the Johnson's workforce would continue to shrink rather than expand. Some women would only work part-time for the firm, and in the summer they found they could earn more money by going fruit-picking, and it was cash in hand with no tax paid. On the other hand, Johnson's were finding that new agreements on holiday pay was adding unforeseen costs to their balance sheets. The new managers forged ahead with their plans, determined to make the remaining factories profitable.

In a large poster entitled *The Johnson Report*, produced just after the sale to Black & Edgington, it was stated, 'The past three months have seen a remarkably swift rationalisation and re-organisation of Johnsons production resources. Although the programme has not been completed, the benefits are already showing through.

For some years, with our two sites in Yarmouth, and our Norwich and Gorleston factories, we had more space than we really needed, and with the recession in our industry we could not justify increasing our production capacity to use the surplus space. As a result of a detailed analysis it was decided on January 16th to close the Gorleston factory, and move the workforce and machines into our North Quay and Admiralty Road premises in Yarmouth.

This mammoth task had to be completed in just nine weeks before our Gorleston lease expired.' This was achieved, it said, by negotiation with the National Union of Tailors and Garment Workers, and through the 'excellent spirit of co-operation throughout our staff.'

It added, 'But this was only achieved by everybody pulling together, and many people cheerfully undertaking many different tasks in addition to their usual work. Above all, moving the machinery and equipment into North Quay and Admiralty Road and getting it all working promptly was a triumph of sustained effort by Ronnie Webb, our Senior Maintenance Engineer, and his team.'

Ronnie Webb confirms that the staff were loyal and hard-working, always willing to do their best for Johnson's: 'We didn't get paid a lot but we were devoted to the company – you were in them days,' he says.

Ronnie had started at Johnson & Sons as an apprentice at Admiralty Road in 1945. He says, 'You didn't get much of a choice, the war was on and you were told where to go.' He did all kinds of manual jobs, stoking the boilers and learning to maintain the equipment and machinery. 'When I went there it was oilskins – if there was any trouble in the ovens you had to go in there and sort it out. You wouldn't be allowed to do it now.'

Ronnie confirms that at first the sewing machines were powered by a steam-driven system, but later it was converted so that electric motors drove the main shafts. 'All the benches were in a line,' he explains, 'there would be three shafts in the room and all the machines came off those. They had a transmitter on each machine; that had a clutch – when the girl put her foot on the pedal it engaged and turned on the machine. When she took her foot off it stopped, it had a brake. As an apprentice your job was to oil all the bearings once a day and if a girl's belt broke or came off the shaft you'd put the belt on. You were more or less "belt boy." Then you progressed, you went on to individual motors.'

For a time Ronnie worked with an older mechanic named Billy Page, who told him that during the wartime air raids, the men had had to move some of the machines down to the cellar as they couldn't be replaced if damaged.

Billy had been born in 1890 in Gorleston and was raised in the notorious Rows of Great Yarmouth. One of seven children, his father was a fisherman and in the 1911 census Billy was aged 20 and already working as a Warehouseman for Johnson's. In 1953 he died suddenly at the age of 62, suffering a heart attack while in mid-conversation with Ronnie Webb.

Ronnie broke off his career at Johnson's and spent a few years at sea, following his family tradition. After completing National Service he then went back to Johnson's in about 1951, and began learning how to fix the machines. He says, 'The old characters said the only thing you want in this game is a trained eye. Don't just dive in and pull it to bits, sit there and watch it work and figure it out. You start to think like a sewing machine. At first a man called Stanley Clark taught me, later I went to Singer's in Glasgow – I went on every course I could go on.'

As a lad Ronnie had been the target for some of the girls' jokes – they would chase him until he went into hiding. But they would also cover for him if he had been drinking at lunchtime, concealing him among the bales of fabric if anyone asked after him. It was, as others said, a family atmosphere, and Ronnie reckons he could 'recognise most of the girls when they were bending over.'

The mechanics learned to modify machines for Johnson's specific uses, such as when they began to change from oilskin to PVC material. At times there was the need for imaginative ideas too: 'On machines like post machines there was a lot of vibration, and things like scissors would keep falling off the girls' tables. One woman got scissors stuck in her ankle, I had to take her to hospital. After that I put magnets on the tables so the scissors would stay put.' Ronnie confirms that accidents were not uncommon, and he would have to drive people to hospital from time to time. 'The odds were stacked against you,' he says – working with machines such as band knives which, he adds, did sever the fingers of more than one colleague. In the accident report books that still exist, cutting room staff and machinists make up most of the entries, and Ronnie himself appears several times.

Right: Ronnie Webb after redundancy servicing an industrial sewing machine of the type used by outworkers at Johnson's.
Photo: David Smith

Ronnie rose up through the ranks to become chief mechanic and under the new owners Black & Edgington he received further training in servicing machines and in new technology. He would travel up to Glasgow where, he says, he and other mechanics from various manufacturers would attend college courses and workshops, but they were not allowed out at night in case the locals took a dislike to them and started a fight. In the daytime they learned about the latest inventions such as 'vortex' needle cooling systems, and 'magic eye' fabric detectors that would automatically cut the thread if no material was present. Everything was becoming automated with a view to speeding up the flow of work and increasing production.

In 1974 at Johnson's the sewing machines had been modified in the shirt department, doing away with the drive shafts that had powered the machines on two rows of benches, and installing individual electric motors: each unit cost £40, and there were 30 machines on each of the benches. This seemed a sound investment as there were Ministry of Defence contracts and overall sales worth almost £190,000 for the first half of 1975, but shirt sales then declined rapidly, as did many of the other lines. Further mistakes occurred including the importing of ready-made shirts which, although cheaper, were of inferior quality.

In the waterproof clothing department, production planning had become a problem – at times they had not ordered enough cloth and haberdashery to meet demand. The firm therefore acquired a Friden Ticketograph machine: a complicated system whereby the machine printed 'control cards' which were tagged onto bundles of fabric, detailing the work needed and the rate of pay. Girls had to tear a strip off the card when they had completed the work, and hand in the strips at the end of the day to be logged for their wages. In theory, with various check-sheets and cross-references, it should have been easier to keep track of orders and quantities, but some jobs took longer than others and some were more urgent, so it was not a complete solution.

In a 1975 board report it was acknowledged that any failure on the part of Johnson's to deliver on time or to the required standard would result in loss of market share, because the competition was becoming ever stronger. Again, price was a key factor but also some of the company's traditional customers were disappearing. Ronnie Webb comments, 'We had been making stuff for the Navy, for miners, even for the clergy – but we lost the Naval contract when there were cutbacks in the Navy. We used to make donkey jackets for miners and then they stopped a lot of the mining.'

When the Johnson's factories began to close, it fell to Ronnie Webb and his team to dismantle, move and even break up the machinery in them. He says, 'I first closed Admiralty Road – I walked through that factory, remembering all them girls and all them machines and the people there – that was heartbreaking. It sent a cold feeling through me. The next one we closed was Gorleston and we moved everything to Yarmouth. I marked every bench and what position that went in, they were all numbered, they all went in a big lorry. I can't remember when I closed the Norwich factory, in Aylsham Way, but we all finished up at the Conge. The families that had worked for Johnson's had all been united and that was being destroyed.' Looking at a photo of a machine used for coating fabric, Ronnie says 'I smashed that up.'

In September 1978 staff received the sad news that Russell Johnson, former chairman and manager of the oilskin works, had died at the age of 69. Countless tributes were paid to him at a large funeral in St Nicholas Church, Great Yarmouth and on a floral display sent by the girls from the factories they had written, 'His life was full of kindly deeds; A helping hand to all our needs; A cheerful smile, a heart of gold, The nicest boss the world could hold.'

The atmosphere was not entirely negative at Johnson's during this time. Ronnie Webb and other members of staff took part in the Caister carnival and also staff entertained local elderly people with a sing-along concert at Christmas.

Meanwhile the managers had introduced a 'Miss Johnson' title – the girls did not have to compete, but each year an attractive young lady would be given the title and would wear a sash and crown for publicity photographs. The title also meant they qualified as entrants to the Yarmouth Carnival Queen contest.

Right: Judith Berry

Unfortunately, David Johnson still did not fit in with the managers' vision and in 1978 it was made clear to him that they would like him to leave. Months of negotiation followed before terms were agreed, and David left the company, bringing an end to the long tradition of family members working at Johnson's. He set himself up as an independent agent and enjoyed many years of success, often dealing with former customers of Johnson & Sons Ltd.

In 1980 ten employees were recognised and rewarded for their long service: between them they had served 325 years with the company. Peggy Driver, Laura Blyth, Phyllis Hewitt, Peter Godbolt and George Nichols had reached the 40-year mark and received watches, while only five could now claim 25 years' service, and they received clocks. They were: Peggy Hastie, Gerty Norton, Rose Norton, Doris Porter and Vivien Winters.

On the following page the group is seen at the presentation which took place in the canteen at the Conge factory, with general manager of Clare's Carlton Mike Smith (far left) who was quoted in the local newspaper as saying that he 'wished them continuing success in their jobs.'

Sadly, this was not to be. Sixty workers were made redundant at the Conge that year, and worse was to come.

Former staff members recall that they were asked to work extra hours around Christmas 1981, to get some important orders completed. At the time few suspected what was to come: in the New Year they were to lose their jobs.

Local newspaper the *Great Yarmouth Mercury* was given the story on the same day that staff were told, and the headline read 'More jobs misery as Yarmouth firm axes 98 workers'. With the town's unemployment rate standing at 14%, this was an unwelcome development. The managing director of Clares Carlton at Yarmouth, Lawson Tolley, said, 'The recession in the textile and clothing industry in general, and a lack of substantial orders, coupled with ever-increasing costs, have resulted in severe losses for the company. The decision to close reflects the need to take drastic measures to centralise their operations at the Wells, Somerset, production unit.' He expressed his regret at the loss of the East Anglian connection.

The factory at the Conge closed on Friday 29th January 1982 and, although a number of staff would find work at Yarmouth Stores, the majority faced an uncertain future. The men and women of Clare's Carlton, formerly Johnson & Sons Ltd, held one, last, farewell party.

Drab Drabbetts.

JACKETS.

Quality.	Single.	Cased.	Lined Collar, check.	Cased and lined.
R38	19/6	23/-	33/-	36/-
R40	21/-	25/-	35/-	39/-
R47	25/-	28/6	39/-	45/-
R65	30/-	34/6	45/-	51/-

Cased and Lined Jackets with hare pockets.

TROUSERS.

Quality.			Unlined.	Lined.
R38	...	...	18/11	25/-
R40	...	...	20/6	28/-
R47	...	...	22/6	30/-
R65	...	...	27/6	34/6

These are made whole falls or fly fronts.

Cooks' Caps.

Shape A	..	4/11	7/6	per dozen.
Shape B	...	4/11	7/6	,,
Cauliflower	...	4/11	7/6	,,

See page 5.

Aprons.

For Painters, Stewards, Butchers, Provision Dealers, &c.

	P5	P6	P8x	P8
Painters' Aprons ...	6/9	7/11	8/9	9/11
Bib and Pocket		Twill.		Dowlas.

	15	30	G89	D14
Stewards' Aprons ...	7/9	8/6	8/11	10/9
Bib, no pockets.				

	Job	W63	W62	F516	A12	510
Butchers' Aprons	11/9	12/6	14/6	9/6	12/6	11/6
Bib or ½-Bib.		Striped Jeans.		White Drill.		Plain Blue.

	7	6	4	5	1
Grocers' Aprons ...	7/11	9/9	8/9	9/11	11/9
Fringed.		White.		Dowlas.	

	S	E	D	N
Butchers' Serge Aprons ...	16/11	21/-	21/-	27/-

	X	XX	1	2
,, (Fleshers' Stripe)	21/-	24/-	30/-	34/6

Pillow Cases.

	C1	C2	C3	C4
White Cotton	3/11	4/6	4/11	5/6 per dozen.

	1	2	3	4
Fancy Check	4/6	4/9	5/3	6/6 ,,

24   JOHNSON & SONS, Ltd., Gt. Yarmouth.

Boiler Suits.

See page 25.

	00	0	BR	96	R	150
Bluette	39/-	42/-	45/-	51/-	60/-	80/-

	D20	P40	360	D27	413	436	509
Dungaree	40/-	42/-	45/-	48/-	51/-	57/-	62/-

	T40	141x	C
Denim (Blue or Brown)	39/-	45/-	51/-

			1
Tan Drabbett	...	...	...	59/-

			142
Tannette	...	...	...	42/-

With Hoods, 4/- to 8/- doz. extra, according to quality.

Bags.

	F1	F2	F3
White Duck	...	9/6	12/6	15/-

	4	5	6	7	8
Canvas ...	12/-	15/11	17/6	21/-	25/-

	44 inch	54 inch
Canvas, No. 1 special	...	25/-	30/-

	F6	36 inch
Twill Cotton	...	7/11	9/6

Tan, Bluette, and Dungaree to order.

Plasterers'.

			T169	T193
Jackets	...	...	22/9	25/6
Aprons	...	...	7/6	9/6

Painters'.

(GREY TWILL).

		C16	C17	C18	C19
Coats	...	27/6	28/6	30/6	33/-

		C14x	C10	C12	C15	C42
Jackets	...	17/6	21/-	24/6	23/6	24/-

					C10	C15
Trousers	...				21/-	22/6

No. C12 double backs and sleeves ; all others single.

Football Knickers.

			126	128
White Drill	...	...	12/6	14/6
			130	132
Dungaree	...	...	13/9	16/6
			134	136
Swansdown	...	...	14/9	18/9

Chesterfield
Butchers' Coats.

A large stock always on hand, with Prussian collar, detachable buttons and rings, and three outside patch pockets.

Flap pockets and F.F., 3d. coat extra.

	A6	A7	A8
Blue Coats ...	42/-	54/-	54/-

	A9	A10	A11	
White Drill Coats	45/-	47/-	57/-	

	A11x	A13	A14	A15
	42/-	47/-	54/-	57/-

		A16	A17
Striped Jean Coats ...	...	47/-	60/-

Assorted lengths, 36 in. to 42 in.

Special attention given to all orders for

Motor Coats & Sleeves

For cleaning.   Made in Holland, Blue Twills, Khaki, and White Drill.

From 4/- upwards.

Warehousemen's Coats

Made in Khaki, and Hollands.

From 3/6 upwards.

Umpire Coats

Made in white (unless ordered otherwise).

From 4/6 upwards.

Fish Salesmen's Coats

Made in Tan and Drab Drabbett.

From 4/11 upwards.

Provision Dealers' Coats

Made in white Drill, or Grey Twill.

From 3/9 upwards.

Special orders are despatched quickly.

Woolette, Grey Tweed, and Grey Flannel Shirts.

Woolette, Red and Black, Black and
White, Fancy Checks, and Stripes ...   18/11 to 24/6

	T50	T51	T65	"SPURN"	T52
Grey Tweed	17/9	21/-	18/11	19/6	22/6

	T53	T55
	23/6	24/6

	T57	T58	T60	KA	Humber
Grey Army Flannel	26/11	26/9	28/6	28/6	28/6

	T61	T62	T63	T64	Best
	35/6	35/6	42/-	45/-	54/-

Also Serge, Linsey, and Swaizeland Shirts.

Matt Cricket and Tennis Shirts.

With Collar and Outside Pocket.

White, from 14/11 to 30/-

Cream Flannelette, all prices.

Fancy Tennis, from 16/11 to 30/-

Customers sending Tabs with orders can have same affixed
free of charge.

Drawers.

Striped Kersey	**300**	**310**	**320**	**330**
	16/9	18/11	21/-	23/-

	340	**350**	**360**	**370**
	25/-	27/6	30/-	33/-

	410	**420**	**430**	**440**	**450**
White Kersey	18/11	21/-	23/-	25/-	27/6

	460	**470**
	30/-	33/-

	00	**01**	**A**	**M1**
Linsey ...	8/11	10/6	12/6	17/9

	T50	**100**	**110**	**120**	**130**
Grey Tweeds ·	12/6	14/9	15/6	16/6	18/6

	140	**150**	**160**	**K.A.**
	19/6	22/6	25/-	19/6

			404	**408**
Grey Sagathy	...	...	18/6	25/-

	500	**505**	**510**	**515**	**520**
Swansdown	12/6	14/6 ·	18/6	21/-	24/-

				24x	**26x**
White Plaiding	...	...		26/9	28/6

———

Also Navy and White Serge, Grey Army Flannel,
Shetland, and Striped Devon, &c.

144

HOSIERY LIST, 1905.

Hand-Knit Navy Guernseys

(INDIGO DYE.)

Boys'	...	47/-	59/-	69/-	—	—
Youths'	...	69/-	76/6	81/-	90/-	—
S. Men's	...	76/6	81/-	9c/-	102/-	108/-
Men's	...	81/-	90/-	102/-	108/-	114/-
O.S. Men's		96/-	99/-	105/-	114/-	126/-
Ex. O.S. Men's		105/-	114/-	126/-	138/-	150/-

Above Seed or Seed and Bar Pattern.

Ribbed Guernseys.

S. Men's	...	...	...	114/-
Men's	...	...	...	126/-

Mersey Guernseys.

(Seed and S. & B.)

S. Men's	...	81/-	93/-	105/-
Men's	...	90/-	102/-	114/-

38 **JOHNSON & SONS, Ltd., Gt. Yarmouth.**

Cable Guernseys.

S. Men's	...	114/-	126/-	—
Men's	...	126/-	138/-	150/-

H.K. Extra Super 4-fold Guernseys.

S. Men's	...	126/-	138/-	150/-
Men's	...	138/-	150/-	162/-

Machine-Knit Navy Guernseys

Boys'	...	...	35/-	42/-	54/-
Youths'	...	...	50/-	57/-	72/-
S. Men's	...	...	57/-	63/-	81/-
Men's	...	...	63/-	69/-	93/-

Seed, Seed and Bar, Cable, and Fancy Patterns.

Boys'	18in.	20in.	22in.	24in.	26in.	28in.	30in.	32in.
F.P.	26/6	29/-	31/6	34/-	36/6	39/-	41/6	44/-

Boot Hose.

Hand-Knit, Abb	...	28/6	31/6	33/-	—	—
Hand Knit, White or Grey					Ex long.
Yarn	...	...	25/-	28/6	31/6	33/-	42/-
Machine-Knit, Abb	...	21/-	—	—	—	—
					Ex. long.
Machine-Knit, Scoured Abb	18/6	22/6	25/6	30/-	33/-

146

Boot Socks.

Machine-Knit, Abb ...	...	...	12/6
Machine-Knit, Scoured Abb	...	...	14/6

Mitts.

Hand-Knit, Abb ...	9/6	10/6	11/6	12/6
Hand-Knit, White or Grey Yarn	8/6		9/6	10/6
Machine-Knit, Grey or Drab Alloa	—		5/6	8/6
Hand-Knit, Navy Worsted	—		10/6	11/6

Abb Drawers.

Hand-Knit, Scoured Abb ...	S. Men's 69/-
	Men's 78/-
Machine-Knit, Scoured Abb	S. Men's 45/-, 49/-
	Men's 49/-, 57/-

Hose.

Heavy Ribbed Navy	12/6	14/6	16/6	21/-	25/-
Heavy Ribbed Grey or Drab Alloa	12/6	14/6	16/6	18/6	
Heavy Ribbed Navy Alloa	18/6				
White ,, Alloa	18/6				
Plain Navy Worsted	9/6	10/6	12/6	14/6	18/6	21/-
Hand-Knit Plain Navy	33/-				

147

52   JOHNSON & SONS, Ltd., Gt. Yarmouth.

Cardigans.

	S. Men's.	Men's.	O.S. Men's.	Ex. O.S. Men's
B4		18/11	21/6	25/-
V.C. 2/6 doz. extra.				
B6		23/6	26/6	31/6
V.C. 3/- doz. extra.				
Corker		28/6	33/-	37/6
V.C. 4/- doz. extra.				
Champion		36/-	42/-	47/-
V.C. 4/- doz. extra.				
B50 Boxed	44/-	45/-	51/-	57/-
V.C. 4/- doz. extra.				
C70 Boxed	54/-	57/-	62/-	68/-
V.C. 5/- doz. extra.				
200 Boxed	81/-	84/-	90/-	96/-
V.C. 6/- doz. extra.				
460 Boxed	93/-	96/-	102/-	108/-
V.C. 6/- doz. extra.				
475 Boxed	105/-	108/-	114/-	120/-
V.C. 6/- doz. extra.				
480 Boxed	120/-	126/-	132/-	141/-
V.C. 7/- doz. extra.				

Heavy Natural Shirts.

		S.M.	M.	O.S.
140½	Unshrinkable	24/-	24/6	28/-
½ sleeves 6d. less.				
141x	Unshrinkable Wool	32/-	33/-	37/-
½ sleeves 6d. less.				
14	Unshrinkable Wool	34/6	35/-	40/-
½ sleeves 6d. less.				
340	Wolsey ditto	46/-	47/-	52/-
½ sleeves 1/- less.				
350	Wolsey ditto	52/-	54/-	60/-
½ sleeves 1/- less.				

Heavy Natural Pants.

140½	Unshrinkable	27/-	27/6	31/-
141x	Unshrinkable Wool	35/-	35/6	39/6
14	„ „	37/6	38/6	42/-
340	Wolsey ditto	60/-	51/-	57/-
350	„	60/-	63/.	69/.

Appendix two: Table showing pre-war and wartime employment and an estimate of post war employment if factory accommodation to replace the buildings destroyed were not available

Factory Premises	1939 no. employed	1940 no. employed after evac.	1941 After destruction of factories	1942	1945 Feb	Remarks	Approx no. after war
Middlegate St Gt Yarmouth	530	Stockport 270	Destroyed	—	—	Total loss	
Hosiery - Row 108-111	80	To Leicester	Destroyed	—	—	Ditto	
Admiralty Road Gt Yarmouth	375	375	Part Destroyed 350	320	285	Factory Act limits no. to 300/320	320
Pier Plain, Gorleston	250	Stockport 90	190	Returned 200	220	Additional space for 30	250
39 High Street Stockport		200	200	120	95	Required by owners	
Bulwer Road, Leicester		50	50	lease terminated			
Sullington, Shepshed			30	30	30	Required by owners	
Total labour	**1235**	**985**	**790**	**670**	**630**		**570**

Appendix three:

A brief history of Yarmouth Stores Ltd

On the 1St February 1898 Johnson & Sons became a limited company, and three days later four of the partners had joined forces with local business associates to form a new company, the Yarmouth Stores Limited. The first directors were John William Budds Johnson, his son William, Arthur Herbert Johnson, his son Frank, their business friends William George Knights and George Wesley Chadd. It was to be a major outlet for Johnson's goods and a lucrative sideline for the family, while Knights and Chadd brought their own successful track record and acumen to the new firm.

William George Knights had been born in 1863 to William Benjamin and Frances Knights – his father had been a mariner and later a lightsman. In the 1881 census the family had been living in Exmouth Road, Great Yarmouth but ten years later all that had changed: Frances had died, William Benjamin was now registered aboard the Corton Light Vessel where he had the job of lamplighter, and his son William George had gone into retailing. In fact William George had also started his own family, having married local girl Emma Mobbs and they had had a son, named William Robert Mobbs Knights, who would be their only child.

In 1891 William George Knights and his family were recorded as living at 70 & 71 South Quay, Great Yarmouth where he ran an outfitter's shop for Johnson & Sons Ltd. Following the death of their mother he had taken his younger brother George to live with him and was training the 14 year old to be a draper's assistant. The family also had a live-in servant, Annie Starling.

This property was leased from the then owner, a Mrs Sarah Lark, by John and Arthur Johnson from 1892 and was later purchased and brought into the business of Yarmouth Stores (see page 17).

Left: the Knights
family – William
George, Emma nee
Mobbs, their son
William Robert and
his wife Nelly

George Wesley Chadd was 20 years older, born into a family with a
long association with the sea. His own father Robert had been a
merchant seaman who had died on Christmas Day in 1850 at the age of
38, not by drowning as his descendants later believed, but having
succumbed to lung disease while on board a ship – his place of death
was given as 'near South Tower, Yarmouth.' He left a widow with four
children still at home, the youngest a newborn baby girl. George at the
age of seven was now the man of the house and in spite of the family
tragedy he became a sailor at the earliest opportunity. In 1867 he married
Victoria Smith Wiseman, a milliner who had been working in the market
place at Great Yarmouth. The family have not been traced in the 1871
census but by the following survey for the year 1881 George had given
up the sea and taken a job as manager in a waterproofs warehouse in
Great Yarmouth, working for Johnson & Sons.

George and his wife were now living in Ordnance Road close to the
sea, but theirs had been far from an idyllic start to married life. They had
produced no children in the first ten years and then their first baby,

whom they named Bertie George, died within a year of his birth. Their next son born in 1879 was named George Bertie, and they had a second son three years later whom they called Victor John. In the meantime Victoria's sister Louisa had died and the couple took charge of her son William Crask.

In 1883 George Chadd purchased land in Bevan Street, Lowestoft on which he was to build a shop and house. *Kelly's Directory* for 1885 lists George as a fishermen's outfitter with premises in Bevan Street and Waveney Road, both conveniently located near to the station and the fish docks. His family are shown living at 133 Bevan Street in the 1891 census, with Victoria's nephew William Crask, now aged 22, working as an outfitter's assistant. The business was doing well enough not only to employ William but also for the Chadds to employ a domestic servant.

Under the terms of the Memorandum of Association dated February 1898 George Chadd leased his Lowestoft property at Bevan Street to the newly formed Yarmouth Stores for 14 years at the rate of £60 per annum. His family moved out to a house in Park Road – George only lived for another eight years, but his sons were ready to follow him into the business.

In the 1898 agreement nominal single shares of £1 each were allocated to the parties involved and then the bulk of the shares were distributed in relation to the investment of the founding partners: 3,654 shares went to John William Budds Johnson and the same to Arthur Herbert Johnson; 1,416 to George Wesley Chadd and 800 to William George Knights. An additional 400 shares were allocated to the chairman, Arthur Johnson.

The objects of the new firm were 'To carry on business as retail outfitters, clothiers, hosiers, fishermen's and seamen's outfitters including boots, shoes, oils, waterproof clothing of every description, drapery, goods of all kinds, and generally to buy and sell and deal in such goods by retail. To carry on business as general warehousemen, ship chandlers, retail dealers in fishermen's requisites of every description: cutch, rope, merchants' grocery and provision including fruit and potatoes and dealers in tobacco and cigars.....'

The brief was broad, but it was firmly rooted in retail, not in manufacturing, although that would later change.

In addition to the shop and warehouse premises in South Quay, Great Yarmouth and in Bevan Street, Lowestoft, the directors took on property in Southgates Road in Great Yarmouth, and they opened stores at Baker Street, Gorleston, at Southside Street, Plymouth, and in Aberdeen. As the business expanded these were followed by new branches in Brixham, Milford Haven, Lerwick, North Shields, Blyth, Newlyn, Grimsby, Hull, Fleetwood and Padstow.

Above: Yarmouth Stores shop in Humber Street, Grimsby c.1900. Company Clerk Joseph Turner is second from the left – photo courtesy of his grandson Donald Turner

Yarmouth Stores began to have a presence all around the British coast, although current chairman and managing director Christopher Knights, comments, 'Some of those properties were no more than shacks on the side of docks... Yarmouth Stores was set up simply to sell everything that was required by the fishing industry.'

To that end, the firm opened its own sheet metal works at Yarmouth, which moved to Corton during the Second World War. Christopher explains, 'Today everything is plastic, but in those days all the items had to be made by tinsmiths and metal workers – they made everything from ships' lamps to pots and pans for use in the galley, metal shapes for ships' signalling, brineometers for measuring the density of brine, shovels and scoops for the herring catch...'

The following pages are from a Yarmouth Stores catalogue from the 1930s:

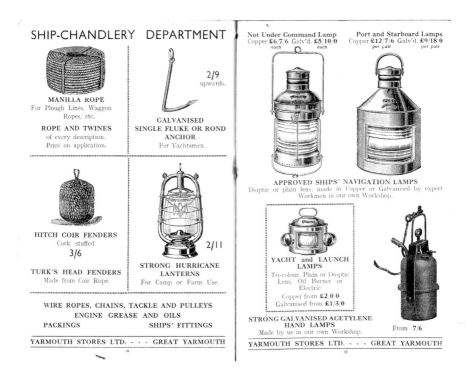

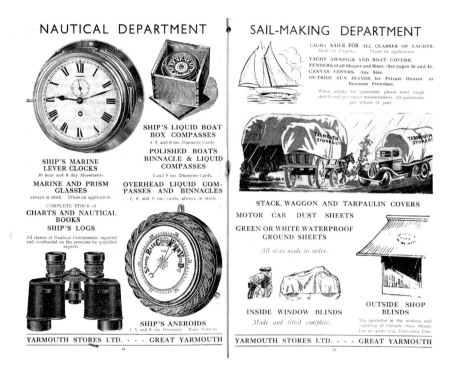

The firm also opened a basket works at Yarmouth, and grew its own willow:

BASKET-MAKING DEPARTMENT

WE ARE ACTUAL MAKERS OF

Swill Baskets	Cane Maunds
Cran Baskets	Bricklayers' Skeps
Riving Maunds	Coal Skeps
Fitch Maunds	Laundry Baskets
Oval Cob Maunds	Travelling Baskets
Washing Maunds	Fancy Baskets
Beet Baskets	Fruit Baskets
Feeding Skeps	Travellers' Sample
White or Brown Eel Pots	Fancy Chairs in Wicker work

Left and below: men at work processing willow and creating basket ware for Yarmouth Stores Ltd

Above: an 80-bushel basket which was made in just two days by expert basket maker Kenneth Blyth (left of picture)

For all its waterproof and protective clothing and work wear items, Yarmouth Stores was supplied by Johnson & Sons Ltd. Catalogues carrying the Johnsons' range were re-labelled for Yarmouth Stores with up to a 50% mark-up on price.

As a minor sideline, Yarmouth Stores Ltd opened a small shop further along South Quay, selling groceries. It is believed that this was partly to provide work for William Knights's father, who had retired from his last job as master of the Dudgeon Light Vessel off Yarmouth, and although he was in receipt of a Trinity House pension he had re-married in 1892 at the age of 48 and had two more children to support.

William died in 1926, and it appears that Yarmouth Stores did not continue with the sale of groceries; their main business was hardware and clothing for the seafaring community.

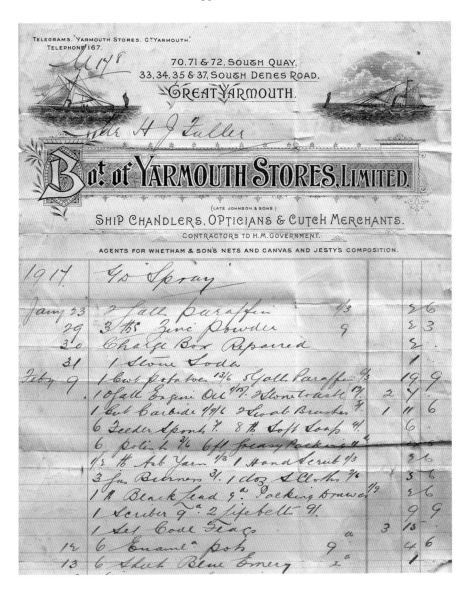

Above: extract of 1917 invoice for items including paraffin, zinc powder, soda, soft soap, polish, black lead and lifebelts. They could also re-calibrate sensitive instruments such as ship's compasses.

In the heyday of the herring fishing industry, Yarmouth Stores would stay open until 11 o'clock at night when the Scottish girls arrived to kit themselves out ready for the arduous and filthy task of sorting, gutting and packing the fish. Oilskin skirts, trousers, aprons and boots were essential wear.

Ladies' Oilskin Skirts

With bib shoulder straps (in BLACK only), waist ties, made from stout rough finish Oilskin. (Yellow to order). In lengths from waist band—30", 32", 34", 36", 38", 40". Single material.

PRICE .... **5/6** EACH.

Double Front and Bib, with pocket in bib. **6/11** each. Postage 7d.

LADIES' HOOD JACKETS

In stout rough-finish Black Oilskin, made to button down front, hood attached to Jacket, with short sleeves.

PRICE ...... **6/6** Postage 6d.
EACH.

Prices from 1930s catalogue

Even at the cost of a few shillings in earlier days, these garments represented a significant investment for the girls who might earn only £10–12 for a whole season's work.[1]

---

[1] The Angus Macleod Archive available at www.angusmacleodarchive.org.uk

One Scottish fisherman appears to have been given an oilskin sample for free – but he threw it away. The story is told in an oral history interview with an old Norfolk drifterman, who was talking about the superstitious nature of the fishermen. He said he had gone to Lerwick with 'Wee Green' in his boat the Ocean Searcher: 'And he went to the Yarmouth Stores to pay up for what he'd had there, you see. Ropes if you wanted or anything. And that poured of rain, and he gives him a black oily coat. Well – we went to sea two or three nights, we never got a – never see a fish. He said, "That's that damned oiler. That's what them buggers give that to me for," he said. He got hold of that and chucked it overboard.' The storyteller said that on the next trip out they pulled out 120 cran of fish, confirming in the fisherman's mind that the oilskin had been at fault.[2]

At the start of the new century there were changes to the board of directors at Yarmouth Stores Ltd: the two elder Johnson brothers died, leaving their majority shareholdings to their sons. In 1906 George Wesley Chadd died and probate was granted to his two sons, with effects valued at over £10,000. Their mother retained the firm's shares but after her passing in 1909 the two sons inherited them. The elder brother, George Bertie, sold his interest in the company to his sibling Victor for £500.[3] George had bought shop premises in London Road North, Lowestoft, and there he concentrated on developing what would become first a much-respected gentlemen's outfitters, and later an impressive local department store with further shops in Southwold, Suffolk. Victor remained as manager of the Lowestoft branches of the company.

With a younger generation now at the helm, the Knights family in particular began to re-consider their business relationship with the Johnsons. Under the terms of the original agreement Yarmouth Stores was obliged to buy its waterproof clothing from Johnson & Sons Ltd, or to seek permission before sourcing stock elsewhere. They could not

---

[2] Thompson, P. Wailey, T & Lummis, T. *Living the Fishing* Routledge 1983 pp 192-3
[3] Chadd., M, *The Story of Chadds, Lowestoft 1907-2000* p7

easily negotiate on price, and by 1935 it was felt that by separating from the Johnsons they could take the business in new directions. Following their buy-out of the Johnson family's stake in Yarmouth Stores Ltd, the Knights family were able to make new plans, which included setting up their own clothing factory. The Johnson and Knights families were now in competition and were no longer on friendly terms.

For both firms the 1930s was a difficult time, with worse to come. As stated in the company's website: '1939 saw the start of the war, and the fishing industry declined drastically. Fishing boats were commandeered by the Admiralty and The Yarmouth Stores turned to working for the war effort, manufacturing for Admiralty contracts throughout the war years. A firebomb hit the factory during a bombing raid over Yarmouth, but luckily it failed to explode. Wartime closed many of the branches, never to be re-opened.'[4]

Not only did the decline in fishing affect the need for clothing, but also for basket ware, and inevitably that side of the business closed. However, in the mid 1960s gas was discovered off the Norfolk coast and a new industry grew rapidly; Yarmouth Stores was quick to respond, supplying the vessels and crews with chandlery, equipment, chemicals and clothing.

William Robert Mobbs Knights had died in 1952 at the age of 65, and his son Kenneth was now running the company. Soon Kenneth's own son Christopher would join the firm. In 1977 the rift between the Johnson and Knights families was bridged when Noel Johnson, finding that he was no longer to be employed in his own firm, contacted Yarmouth Stores and offered his services. Old differences were put aside and he joined the company on a part-time basis, bringing with him a great deal of experience, and a number of former Johnson's customers.

At this time the factory was expanded and a new shop and head office was built on the South Quay site. Christopher Knights said, 'the factory premises was probably doubled or trebled in size. Noel oversaw

---

[4] The Yarmouth Stores website at www.yarmo.co.uk

the factory and acted as manager; he would negotiate the contracts and bring in new business. He was with us until the end of his life – he would come in every day, even when his health was failing, right up until he went into hospital.'

Christopher adds 'He was always very interested in the staff, in the people: he would walk around and talk to everyone, he was a people's person. When Noel joined us the number of machinists increased to about 50 – there had been about a dozen when I joined, but in the 60s and 70s we did very well as the oil industry took off.'

As staff at Johnson's became disenchanted with the new management there, a number of them applied to join the Yarmouth Stores team instead, and when Johnson's finally closed in 1982 many of the machinists were looking for work. Doris Porter was one of those who made the move to South Quay. She said, 'I started on the machine then later I was put in charge of the factory. We were making a lot of the same things as Johnson had been – I think Noel got a lot of customers to go with him.'

The flourishing market enabled further expansion in 1985 when the ship chandlery side of the business was moved to new, larger premises in Friars Lane. In Southgates Road the old building was pulled down in 1989 and replaced with a purpose-built oil warehouse.

Yarmouth Stores Ltd celebrated its centenary in 1998, having weathered the changing fortunes of the fishing and shipping industries for a hundred years. Moving into the 21st century Christopher Knights and his management team knew that they would have to remain adaptable in order to respond to new opportunities and needs, seeking out new customers both at home and overseas, whether for work or leisure wear, or tools and equipment for industries such as the building trade and the recently-emerged renewable energy market, such as the building of wind farms around and off the East coast. Embracing technologies such as selling via the internet helps to make Yarmouth Stores products available world wide, and, it is hoped, customers may be able to appreciate them for another hundred years to come.

Clothing for the Working
& Leisure Environment